D0783323

Slim Forever
The French Way

Slim Forever
The French Way

Michel Montignac

For more information, visit the
Montignac Universal Official Website
at **www.montignac.com** or the
Montignac Boutique & Café website
at **www.montignac.co.uk**

Project Editor Shannon Beatty
Project Designer Jo Grey
Senior Editor Jennifer Jones
Project Art Editor Sara Robin
Managing Editors Stephanie Farrow, Penny Warren
Managing Art Editor Marianne Markham
Publishing Manager Gillian Roberts
Art Director Carole Ash
Publishing Director Mary-Clare Jerram
DTP Designer Sonia Charbonnier
Production Controller Elizabeth Warman
Photographer Kate Whitaker
Canadianizer Christine Heilman
Editor, Canada Julia Roles

First Canadian Edition 2005
Copyright © 2005, 2007 Dorling Kindersley Limited
Text copyright © 2005, 2007 Michel Montignac

Dorling Kindersley is represented in Canada by
Tourmaline Editions Inc, 622 King Street West, Suite 304
Toronto, Ontario M5V 1M7

Every effort has been made to ensure that the information contained in
this book is complete and accurate. However, neither the publisher nor
the author is engaged in rendering professional advice or services to the
individual reader. Professional medical advice should be obtained for
specific information on personal health matters. Neither the publisher nor
the author accept any legal responsibility for any personal injury or other
damage or loss arising from the use or misuse of the information and
advice in this book.

All rights reserved. No part of this publication may be reproduced, stored
in a retrieval system, or transmitted in any form or by any means,
electronic, mechanical, photocopying, recording, or otherwise without the
prior written permission of the copyright owners.

Library and Archives Canada Cataloguing in Publication

Montignac, Michel
Slim Forever the French Way / Michel Montignac-- Canadian ed.

Includes index
ISBN:-13: 978-1-55363-084-5
ISBN:-10: 1-55363-084-X
1. Reducing diets   2 Glycaemic index   I. Title.

RM222 2M557   615.2'83   C2005-902404-6

Color reproduction by GRB, Italy
Printed and bound by South China Printing Co. Ltd (China)

07 08 09 10 9 8 7 6 5 4 3 2

Discover more at
www.dk.com

Contents

Foreword

Twenty years ago, when I published my first book on weight watching, losing weight was basically an aesthetic concern. In 1997, however, after the World Health Organization raised the alarm and decreed that obesity was a health risk and that it had become an epidemic affecting people worldwide, weight control became a public health consideration.

Meanwhile, long before the end of the second millennium, nutritionists and other diet authorities had started to address this problem. For 50 years, they had been trying to make us feel guilty by telling us that if we were overweight, it was simply because we ate too much (consumed too many calories), particularly fats, and did not exercise enough. However, more recently published epidemiological studies indicate exactly the contrary. These studies show that, since 1960, people in the West have been reducing their daily caloric intake (particularly fats) by 25 to 35 percent and that, paradoxically, obesity has risen by 400 percent during the same period.

Hundreds of scientific studies carried out during the past 25 years show that our hormones, and not calories, are at the heart of obesity. The true functional cause is hyperinsulinism—a chronic and excessive secretion of insulin, a key metabolic hormone—and this condition is the last stage of a metabolic chain reaction triggered by certain foods—principally high-glycemic carbohydrates.

Throughout the past several decades, "the dietary landscape" in Western societies has changed considerably. To begin with, new and often highly processed foods, practically unknown to our ancestors, have been progressively and insidiously

Right, opposite: on this diet you can eat cheese and drink wine and still lose weight.

introduced into our food chain, to the point of becoming an essential part of our daily lives. Furthermore, the transformation of our everyday food through industrial processing and production has significantly modified the quality of the food we consume.

The nature of the food we eat nowadays stimulates metabolic reactions that channel this food into fatty reserves and jeopardize our bodies' normal energy-burning processes. This is why, on the basis of numerous scientific studies, I have designed a dietary model aimed at teaching people to choose those foods that trigger metabolic responses that allow our bodies to burn food as energy instead of storing it as fat.

Although this applies to all food categories, we have to bear in mind that our choice of carbohydrates is decisive here. Unfortunately, misconceptions regarding carbohydrates remain rife, despite evidence over the past 25 years that the notion of slowly digested carbohydrates and rapidly digested carbohydrates is erroneous, since there is no physiological basis for this belief. As far as our metabolism is concerned, there is no real distinction between "simple" and "complex" carbohydrates. Scientifically, the only criterion that serves to distinguish one carbohydrate from another is its glycemic index (GI). This concept is not widely known, even though it was proven to be true over 25 years ago.

I had the opportunity to hit upon this concept while the eminent diabetes scientists who discovered it were struggling to have it accepted in their domain, where it is still only marginally taken into consideration. I thus decided to apply this concept to weight loss. The results of my experiments were so extraordinary that it became the key element in my recommendations on nutrition. I thus had the honor of

"the only criterion that serves to distinguish one carbohydrate from another is its glycemic index (GI)."

becoming the first author in the world to propose the concept of the glycemic index in relation to weight loss. Many other diet books have followed on my heels. But because they have a lack of background in the GI area, they often broadcast distorted, and even incorrect, information.

For decades, overweight people have listened to official dieticians, who recommend counting calories and following a low-fat diet, which has proven to be a total failure. Inspired by the Atkins diet, several opinion leaders have in recent years declared carbs the real evil. They have switched from one extreme to the other, recommending very low-carb diets. However, people quickly become bored eating this way and may develop cardiovascular problems in the long term. This is why my eating plan is the only perfectly balanced diet. It suggests the right carbs and the right fats.

The goal of this book is to give people who wish to lose weight unbiased information regarding an original nutritional concept that has not only proven to be extremely effective but has also time and again been confirmed by subsequent scientific studies.

I wish you an enlightening discovery.

Michel Montignac

> "my eating plan is the only perfectly balanced diet. It suggests the right carbs and the right fats."

WHY IT WORKS

THE YO-YO EFFECT

The so-called yo-yo effect describes the invariable outcome of low-calorie diets. It refers to the uncontrollable up and down of a dieter's weight after he or she returns to a normal caloric intake. This occurs because low-calorie diets can reduce the basal metabolic rate (the rate at which the body uses calories when at rest) by up to 50 percent, which translates into fast and significant weight gain when normal eating habits are resumed.

The calorie myth

The low-calorie approach to losing weight is based on a simple model that ignores the complexity of the human metabolism. At best it is simplistic; at worst it is dangerous because it can permanently undermine your health. Look around and you will see that the plump, the portly, even the obese, are precisely those who count their calories with the greatest fervor.

THE BOILER METAPHOR

Nutritionists tend to portray the body as a boiler using up energy in the form of calories. If the calories eaten exceed the calories used by the body, then we gain weight. The calories not "burned" by the body are stored as body fat. The problem with this model is that it ignores the way the body uses calories. Contrary to what many people believe, obese people do not eat more calories than slim people. Medical studies have shown the difference in calorific intake between slim, average, and overweight people is, most of the time, insignificant.

The survival instinct

Anyone who has ever followed a low-calorie diet knows that there is an initial period of quick weight loss. This is because the body is accustomed to receiving a certain number of calories and when this number decreases, the body will use an alternative source, such as body fat, to make up the difference. Early weight loss is followed by a plateau, and most of us find it impossible to maintain our weight in the long term.

In response to receiving less food, the body responds as though it has been threatened with starvation, and gradually reduces its energy output so that it will not have to use fat reserves for energy in the future. The result is that the body's basal metabolic rate (the rate at which the body uses energy when at rest) decreases by as much as 50 percent and no further weight loss occurs. In other words, low-calorie diets actually slow down your metabolism (*see chart, below*). This reduced basal metabolic rate leaves your body vulnerable to rapid and excessive weight gain once you come off the low-calorie diet.

Formula for obesity

In the Western world, the low-calorie approach to weight loss has become a part of our culture, institutionalized at every level despite the fact that a reduction in calories can drastically lower metabolic activity. This means that after following a low-calorie diet, any return to normal caloric intake will bring about weight gain.

The sad paradox is that the more you try to reduce your calorie intake, the faster you will put on weight after you come off your diet. In addition, people who embark on low-calorie diets often suffer from fatigue and an impaired immune system, leaving them susceptible to infection and illness. My diet plan, which does not require you to weigh or measure quantities, offers you a better, less restrictive way to lose weight permanently.

"the plump, the portly, even the obese, are precisely those who count their calories with the greatest fervor."

The cross of the undernourished

This graph shows the history of a woman starting with an average daily caloric intake of 2,800. Before going on her first diet, her weight is a stable 220 lb (100 kilograms). As you can see, each time she goes on a low-calorie diet, she goes through a cycle of losing, stabilizing, and regaining her weight. Each successive diet is accompanied by a small weight gain beyond her initial weight. After a few low-calorie diets, she must subsist on less than 1,000 calories a day and weighs more than 243 lb (110 kilograms).

weight in lb/kg	NORMAL DIET	1ST DIET	2ND DIET	3RD DIET	4TH DIET
243 lb (110 kg)					
198 lb (90 kg)					
	2,800 cal	2,000 cal	1,500 cal	1,000 cal	800 cal

Where does the weight come from?

People gain weight not because they eat too much, but because they eat the wrong foods, which in turn wreak havoc on the body in the form of obesity, diabetes, and cardiovascular disease. Undoubtedly, the strong culinary traditions of the French have made it easier for them to resist the insidious spread of the fast-food eating culture and lifestyle.

THE CARBOHYDRATE CONNECTION

In the war on weight, the only food group that really concerns us is carbohydrates, and they are the main subject of this book. Carbohydrates are made up of units of sugar (*for more on carbohydrates, see pp32–37*). Insulin, a hormone secreted by the pancreas, plays a vital role in the metabolism of carbohydrates.

During digestion, the sugars in carbohydrates are broken down into simple sugars, mainly glucose, which is then absorbed into the bloodstream. Glycemia is the scientific term for the amount of glucose in the blood, or blood sugar level.

The presence of glucose in the bloodstream triggers the pancreas to release insulin, which enables glucose to pass from the blood into the cells of the body. Once it is in the cells, glucose is burned together with oxygen to create energy.

In a healthy person's body, any excess glucose is converted into glycogen (a complex carbohydrate), which is held in the muscles and liver as a short-term energy reserve. During the course of the day, and specifically between meals when our energy reserves start to drop, the pancreas triggers the hormone glucagon to turn glycogen back into glucose. This process ensures that the body maintains a steady blood sugar level throughout the day.

"the strong culinary traditions of the French have made it easier for them to resist the insidious spread of the fast-food eating culture and lifestyle."

The hyperglycemic-hypoglycemic cycle

When you eat high-sugar carbohydrates, it destabilizes your blood sugar levels and traps your body into a vicious circle of hyperglycemia and hypoglycemia. This happens because eating a high-sugar carbohydrate causes the level of sugar, or glucose, in your blood to rise far above normal. This is called hyperglycemia. In response, your pancreas floods the bloodstream with insulin. This, usually excessive, amount of insulin drives the glucose out of the bloodstream, which results in blood sugar levels falling far below normal. This state, known as hypoglycemia, makes you feel hungry and shaky, which prompts you to reach for a high-sugar snack, and the cycle begins again.

Eat high-sugar food, which triggers a spike in blood sugar level (hyperglycemia)

High blood sugar level stimulates the pancreas to secrete a large amount of insulin

Body feels shaky, so you reach for a high-sugar snack

Excess insulin drives too much sugar, or glucose, out of the bloodstream

Lack of glucose causes significant drop in blood sugar level (hypoglycemia)

PASTA

Spaghetti, depending on what it is made from and how it is cooked, can be either a high-sugar carbohydrate or a low-sugar one. If you always choose pasta in its least glycemic form (*see pp64–65*), it will not lead to high blood sugar levels, or hyperglycemia.

So where does it all go wrong?

As we have seen, eating carbohydrates causes the level of sugar in the bloodstream to rise. The pancreas, in response, will secrete insulin to bring blood sugar levels back to normal. However, when we eat carbohydrates with a high sugar release potential (*see pp18–21*), they send blood sugar levels soaring far above normal in a relatively short space of time. This is a state known as hyperglycemia. This triggers the pancreas to release a large amount of insulin to bring blood sugar levels down to normal. Any excess glucose is stored as glycogen, but once the glycogen stores are full, any remaining glucose is stored as fat.

If excess insulin is produced, it will rapidly drain the glucose from the blood, and this can result in abnormally low blood sugar. This is a state known as hypoglycemia. The symptoms of hypoglycemia can include chronic fatigue, lack of concentration, intense hunger, and irritability. Those experiencing low blood sugar levels tend to reach for a sugary snack to feel better. This will cause high blood sugar levels, which trigger a large production of insulin. This results in hyperglycemia. The vicious circle (*see chart, p15*) then starts all over again and this in the long term can lead to poor pancreatic function and chronic insulin overproduction known as hyperinsulinism.

Obesity and hyperinsulinism

What distinguishes the person who is overweight from the person who is slim is that the latter has a pancreas secreting just the right amount of insulin to bring a raised blood sugar level down to its normal values. The overweight person does not. Instead of releasing the right amount of insulin, the pancreas will secrete more—sometimes much more—insulin than is required to take sugar present in the blood down to its normal level. This is a metabolic disorder known as hyperinsulinism.

In hyperinsulinism, the whole metabolism is geared toward producing fat with a subsequent increase in fat reserves. Insulin also indirectly inhibits the breakdown of fat. Researchers in nutrition have demonstrated that the degree to which people are overweight is directly linked to the severity of their hyperinsulinism. From this we can reasonably conclude that the only real difference between someone who is slim and someone who is overweight is that the overweight person suffers from hyperinsulinism, while the slim person does not.

From my own research into diabetes and the glycemic index (GI), which is a system for measuring the sugar release potential of carbohydrates (*see pp18–21*), and from my own experience of losing weight by eating low-GI foods, I have concluded that obesity could only be the result of hyperinsulinism. In other words, if you eliminate high-GI carbohydrates from your diet, and replace them with low-GI carbohydrates, it will not only suppress hyperinsulinism, but it will also trigger weight loss.

> "if your pancreas is performing under par, so is your metabolism."

Pancreas health check

Most of us know people who consistently eat high-GI foods and remain slim all their life, despite their bad eating habits. This is because they are blessed with a very healthy pancreas that has not lapsed into hyperinsulinism, regardless of the heavy damage inflicted on it over a long period of time.

This is a dwindling minority of the population, though. If you're reading this book, the chances are that this does not apply to you. It is more likely that you, like the vast majority of others, fall into one of the two following camps.

Poor eating habits?

The first (and more common) pancreatic condition is one that develops over the years. Most of us start off with a healthy pancreas that enables us to stay slim for many years, despite bad eating habits. And then, at the age of about 30 or 35, and certainly by the age of 40, we start to put on weight. In later years, some of us even become obese and diabetic.

The pancreas holds out for several decades, but in the end it succumbs to the abuse it has suffered.

An inherited problem?

The other scenario includes those, like me, who arrived on earth with a substandard pancreas that was inherited. If your parents are overweight (and therefore hyperinsulinic), your chances of having a frail pancreas are high. If your diet from an early age included high-GI foods, it is almost certain that your pancreas is glucose-sensitive, and therefore very unhealthy. And, as we have seen, if your pancreas is performing under par, so is your metabolism.

Both of the two scenarios mentioned above result in weight gain, and no low-calorie diets or punishing exercise regimen will yield sustainable results. The solution lies in normalizing your pancreas and the way it responds to glucose in the bloodstream by eliminating high-sugar foods.

The Glycemic Index

This is a ranking system that measures how much glucose, or sugar, is absorbed into the bloodstream after eating a carbohydrate. Each carbohydrate is assigned a number on the glycemic index, or GI. The number indicates what proportion of the food's total sugar content is absorbed into the bloodstream. The higher the number, the greater the proportion. For instance, lentils have a low GI because only 25 percent of their sugar content is absorbed.

HOW IS IT MEASURED?

Carbohydrate foods contain energy, but not all of this energy is absorbed during the digestive process. Instead of measuring the calories, or potential energy, present in carbohydrates, scientists began to measure the amount of energy, or sugar, actually absorbed from carbohydrates by the body (known as the sugar release potential of a carbohydrate). This is done by measuring the level of glucose in the bloodstream after eating a carbohydrate. The glycemic index is based on the glycemic value for glucose, which is arbitrarily set at 100. As you might expect, though, most foods have GI values below this level.

Why carbohydrates?

Carbohydrates are the only group of foods that are made up of sugars, and therefore the glycemic index only measures the GI values of carbohydrates. Fats and proteins (*see pp22–31*) contain very little, if any, sugar. The impact of fats and proteins on blood sugar levels is negligible, and therefore the glycemic index does not apply to these foods.

The "bad" carbohydrates

These are carbohydrates that produce a large rise in blood sugar levels, such as potatoes, white bread, white rice, and other refined foods. They have a high GI value (above 50). The body is suddenly in a state of

"If you are overweight, you are probably addicted to bad carbohydrates."

WHAT IS A GOOD GI?

Different sources will tell you different things, but on this diet, I use four distinct bands to classify the GI values of carbohydrates. Low- and very low-GI foods are good carbohydrates, while high- and very high-GI foods are bad carbohydrates.

• **very low** (GI of 35 or below)
Will result in weight loss.
Foods include vegetables, such as as cabbage (*see left*), cauliflower, broccoli, zucchini, eggplant, spinach; fruits such as apples, pears, peaches, and cherries; grains and legumes, such as lentils, wild rice, and quinoa.

• **low** (GI of 36–50)
Will prevent weight gain.
Foods include sweet potatoes, brown rice, unrefined basmati rice, whole-wheat pasta, white spaghetti cooked *al dente*, whole-wheat bread, kiwi fruit, and grapes.

• **high** (GI of 51–65)
May result in weight gain.
Foods include overcooked white pasta, raisins, corn, refined semolina, and jam made with sugar.

• **very high** (GI above 65)
Will result in weight gain.
Foods include white bread, sticky white rice, rice cakes, white potatoes, popcorn, and cornflakes.

hyperglycemia, where glucose is raised above its normal level. This stimulates the pancreas to secrete excess insulin, which can lead to fat storage and hypoglycemia.

The "good" carbohydrates

Within this diet's framework, good carbohydrates are those foods that have a small effect on blood sugar levels. These carbohydrates are assigned relatively low numbers (50 and below) on the glycemic index. They cause only a slight rise in blood sugar, which stimulates a small insulin response from the pancreas. These low-GI foods include many types of fruits and cruciferous vegetables, legumes, such as lentils, and whole-grain cereals.

In both the long and short term, low-GI foods will result in the stabilization of blood sugar levels. This, in turn, will help to desensitize the pancreatic response to glucose. This translates into weight loss or weight maintenance, increased energy, and a general sense of well-being.

Fiber: it's not just sugar content that counts

The amount of sugar a carbohydrate contains is not the only thing that affects its GI value. The GI of a food is also affected by the amount of fiber it contains. This is because fiber reduces the amount of sugar the body can absorb from a carbohydrate. For example, an apple is a carbohydrate that contains sugar in the form of glucose, sucrose, and fructose. It also contains a soluble fruit fiber known as pectin. This fiber actually reduces the amount of sugar absorbed from the apple by the body. In essence, the apple's fiber content reduces its GI value.

What about refined foods?

The commercial preparation, or refining, of a carbohydrate can raise a carbohydrate's GI value significantly. When foods are refined, they are stripped of nutrients that reduce the amount of sugar that is absorbed into the bloodstream, such as fiber. For example, the GI of brown rice is 50, which makes it a good, low-GI carbohydrate. When brown rice undergoes the refining process, it becomes white rice. The new GI of the refined,

"You can reduce the GI of an overcooked starch by letting it cool, and eating it cold."

white rice is 70—that's 20 points higher than unrefined, brown rice. The reason for this is that when brown rice is refined into white rice, its fiber has been removed, leaving only starch (a form of carbohydrate) behind. The same thing happens when brown whole-wheat flour is refined into white flour: all of its fiber is removed, and the GI goes up significantly.

In their new, refined forms, both of these foods now more closely resemble glucose. This allows sugar to pass more easily into the bloodstream, since the body has little work to do in order to break the food down into glucose. Once refined, a good carbohydrate can become a bad one, since most of its complex molecular bonds have been broken in the process.

What about cooking foods?

There are other interesting facts to emerge from the adoption of the glycemic index. Cooking can weaken the molecular bonds in some starchy carbohydrates, yielding an effect on GI values similar to refining a food. Two main offenders are potatoes (*see box, right*) and carrots.

When raw, a carrot is a good carbohydrate with a low GI of about 30. However, when it is cooked, either by boiling, grilling, or steaming, its molecular bonds are broken down, which makes it easier for the body to absorb its sugars and convert it into glucose.

When cooked, the carrot's GI jumps 55 points, from 30 to 85, which makes it a bad carbohydrate. Before you worry too much, I can tell you that this really only affects starchy carbohydrates, such as rice and pasta (*see pp54–57*). The best way to limit the damage is to never overcook these foods, and avoid potatoes and corn completely, particularly when you are on the Rapid Weight Loss plan.

However, if you do happen to overcook a starch, such as pasta or rice, do not despair: all is not lost. You can reduce the GI of an overcooked starch by letting it cool, and eating it cold. For example, when overcooked spaghetti has been allowed to cool, its GI will actually go down (by up to five points) through a process known as retrogradation. This applies to almost any overcooked starch, excluding carrots, potatoes, and corn.

POTATOES

The white potato is a good example of how the cooking process can sometimes make a good carbohydrate into a bad one. When raw, a potato is undoubtedly a good, low-GI carbohydrate. Unfortunately, humans cannot digest it when raw. When it is boiled in its skin, however, the GI of a potato shoots up to 65. Mashed potatoes have an even higher GI value of 80. Frying a potato raises its GI even further, to 95. The bottom line: completely omit white potatoes from your diet if you want to lose weight.

Proteins

Proteins are the essential building blocks of human body cells, but did you know that they can also facilitate weight loss? This is because the digestion of protein foods, such as meat and fish, involves an increased expenditure of energy. When the body metabolizes protein, it uses up more energy than when it digests fats or carbohydrates. Protein also provides satiety, which means it leaves you feeling fuller for longer, so you will be less inclined to overeat at meals or to snack between them.

CHOOSE WISELY

Be careful, even suspicious, of all of the foods you put into your body, even proteins. Be wary of farmed fish, since they are bred in captivity and fed industrially produced, high-GI foods. In oily fish, this can translate into a reduced quality of omega-3 fatty acids (see p29).

Similarly, you should also beware of processed meats, such as packaged turkey and ham, which are sweetened with glucose. Fresh milk products that still contain milk water (lactoserum or whey) may also yield an increased insulin response, despite their low GI values. This is why it is best to avoid eating too many fresh dairy products. Instead, it is preferable to eat aged or fermented cheese, as French people do.

Montignac on proteins

Proteins are organic substances found in a wide variety of animal and vegetable foods, including foods such as meat, fish, dairy products, and legumes. They are essential to the body, and since they contain little, if any, sugar, they will not raise your blood sugar levels, stimulate insulin production, or contribute to weight gain.

THE PROTEIN–WEIGHT LOSS CONNECTION

Protein is not only essential for good health, but increasing your daily intake can also facilitate weight loss. The reasons for this are twofold: first, the digestion of protein involves an expenditure—metabolizing protein uses up energy more effectively than metabolizing other foods.

Second, protein leaves you feeling satiated, or fuller, for longer. Feeling satisfied curbs your appetite, which allows you to better control the quality and quantity of the food you eat. It is essential, however, to drink six to eight 8-oz glasses (1.5 to 2 liters) of water each day to eliminate body waste, such as urea, uric acid, and lactic acid created by the metabolism of protein.

How much do you need?

For good health, getting an adequate amount of protein in your diet is absolutely essential. For weight maintenance, a good rule of thumb is to eat at least one gram of protein for each 2.2 pounds (1 kg) of body weight. This is the amount of protein necessary to compensate for losses caused in the renewal of body cells and to prevent possible wasting of muscle tissue.

This means that if you weigh 154 pounds (70 kg) and you want to maintain your weight, you should consume at least 70 grams of protein per day. When your aim is to lose weight, however, you should increase your protein intake to 1.5 grams per 2.2 pounds (1 kg) of body weight per day. So, this means that to lose weight, you should consume at least 105 grams of protein per day, but see your doctor if you have a chronic health condition before increasing the amount of protein you eat. This ensures that your protein intake exceeds the amount necessary for simple tissue renewal, and it will minimize muscle loss. This will prevent a decrease in your basal metabolic rate (*see pp12–13*), since muscle is actually a metabolically active tissue that burns calories, even while you are resting.

Ideal protein options

The best protein sources for weight loss are foods that are low in fat and high in amino acids (*see box, right*). These include low-fat or fat-free cheeses, eggs, fish, and lean meats, such as skinless chicken or skinless turkey.

Although protein does facilitate weight loss, not all protein is ideal. Some meats, such as beef, pork, and poultry (with the skin on), can be high in saturated fats (*see pp26–31*). When eaten in excess (more than a few times per week), the saturated fats contained in these foods can contribute to cardiovascular disease, or the narrowing of blood vessels. These foods can also trigger weight gain when coated in bread crumbs or eaten with high-GI carbohydrates, since the insulin these foods elicit can "trap" the fat in the body (*see below*).

How should I prepare my protein?

The goodness of your protein also depends on how the food is prepared. Lean cuts of meat and fish are healthy protein options, but what you do to it does make a difference. For example, almost any type of fish, whether it is tuna, salmon, or cod, is a healthy source of protein when it is broiled, baked, or steamed. The same is true of lean cuts of beef and pork, and skinless poultry.

However, if you take that same piece of protein and coat it with bread crumbs or flour, it can lead to weight gain. This is not because of the protein itself, but because of the high-GI carbohydrates contained in the bread crumbs or flour. These foods are high-GI carbohydrates, and they will cause a spike in blood sugar levels. This, in turn, will trigger the pancreas to release a large amount of insulin.

COMPLETE PROTEINS

Proteins contain large numbers of amino acids, which are used to make cells. Some of these amino acids are made by the body, while others must be obtained from food. There are no vegetable proteins that contain a complete and balanced amount of amino acids, and the lack of one essential amino acid can interfere with the absorption of another.

This is why it is essential to eat both animal and vegetable proteins; a diet consisting of just vegetable proteins will lack some essential amino acids. Vegetarians should include egg (*see below*) and milk protein in their diets, in addition to vegetable proteins such as soy products. Likewise, meat-eaters should incorporate vegetable protein into their diet to avoid nutritional deficiencies.

Fats

Fats are complex molecules that store energy for long-term use by the body, but fats don't necessarily make you fat! The key to losing and maintaining weight on this diet is to avoid eating carbohydrates that have high GI values. Since fats, such as olive oil, contain little, if any, sugar, their GI values are often negligible. This means that when fats are eaten on their own, they will not elicit an insulin response and therefore they will not contribute to weight gain.

Montignac on fats

Fats, or lipids, are divided into two broad categories, according to their origin. Fats of animal origin are found in meats, fish, butter, cheese, and cream, while fats of vegetable origin include foods such as margarine and olive oil. Rich in a number of vitamins (A, D, E, and K) as well as linoleic acid and linolenic acid (also known as essential fatty acids), fats play a necessary role in a healthy diet when eaten in moderation.

DIFFERENT TYPES OF FATS

Fats can be divided into two main categories: saturated fats and unsaturated fats. Saturated fats are usually derived from animal sources, including meat, butter, cream, and cheese. These fats are solid at room temperature, and they are often thought of as bad fats, since they can increase blood cholesterol levels and contribute to heart disease.

The other category is unsaturated fats. These fats mostly come from fish and vegetable sources, and are liquid at room temperature. They are considered healthier than saturated fats, since they protect the body against heart disease. Some unsaturated fats actually reduce levels of bad blood cholesterol (also known as low density lipids, or LDL), which cause narrowing of the arteries, while simultaneously increasing levels of good blood cholesterol (also known as high density lipids, or HDL). HDL removes built-up cholesterol from the arterial walls, flushing it out of the body. This reduces total blood cholesterol levels.

Unsaturated fats

There are two main types of unsaturated fats: monounsaturated fats are found in vegetable fats, such as avocados, olive oil, and sunflower oil, and have little effect on blood cholesterol. Polyunsaturated fats are found in oily fish such as salmon, fresh tuna, and mackerel, and they can actually lower total blood cholesterol levels (*see above*). Neither of these

"a meal consisting of steak and fries is heresy!"

fats will contribute to weight gain. This is because unsaturated fats, particularly those found in fish, are structurally dissimilar to human fat, and the body must therefore work to convert these types of fat into body fat tissue.

Saturated fats and carbohydrates

As mentioned earlier, eating saturated fats can raise blood cholesterol levels and contribute to the development and progression of heart disease. But if you eat saturated fat together with a high-GI food, the combination can be doubly dangerous for your health and your waistline. When saturated fats are combined with carbohydrates with a GI above 50, they interfere with the way the body digests fat and, as a result, body fat reserves may be laid down. This is because saturated fats are similar in structure to human fat tissue. The insulin response from the high-GI carbohydrate traps the fat that has been eaten.

So remember, a meal consisting of steak and fries is heresy! Meat, of course, contains unsaturated fat, and potatoes are a high-GI carbohydrate. The high levels of insulin circulating in the bloodstream caused by eating the potatoes will ensure that the fat from the steak will be deposited in your body as fatty tissue. The ultimate result will be weight gain. What's more, the weight you gain will be proportional to the quantity of fat consumed with the meal.

Eat fat and stay slim

If you do not have a history of high cholesterol, there is no need to be alarmed about saturated fat. It is bad for your heart, but when eaten in moderation, it will not cause you to gain weight. On this diet, it is perfectly acceptable to eat reasonable amounts of saturated fats, so long as you do not eat them with high-GI carbohydrates (a GI above 50). When eating a meal that contains saturated fats, you must restrict your carbohydrate choices to foods with a GI value of 50 or below. This is because low-GI carbohydrates, including legumes and other vegetables, will only stimulate the pancreas to produce a small amount of insulin, which is not enough to trap and store the fat in the body.

OMEGA-3 FATTY ACIDS

Oily or fatty fish, such as salmon, sardines, herring, and tuna, contains polyunsaturated omega-3 fatty acids, which have various protective and therapeutic properties. Omega-3 fatty acids are particularly good for the heart. I recommend eating as much fatty fish as possible, since it will never contribute to weight gain.

HEALTHY FATS

If you are concerned about heart disease, you should replace saturated fats (found in animal fats, such as butter) in your diet with unsaturated varieties. Unsaturated fats, including oil made from sunflowers (*see left*), can help protect against cardiovascular disease by increasing your good cholesterol levels (*see pp28–29*), while reducing bad cholesterol.

High levels of triglycerides (the main form of fat in adipose tissue), also known as hypertriglyceridemia, can also contribute to cardiovascular disease. This condition can be caused not only by eating saturated fats, but also by consuming high-GI carbohydrates. So a diet rich in unsaturated fats and low-GI carbohydrates can significantly reduce triglyceride levels, bad cholesterol levels, and your risk of cardiovascular disease.

Carbohydrates

All sugars and starches are carbohydrates.
After being transformed into glucose, the sugar and
starches from the carbohydrates are absorbed into the
bloodstream within 30 minutes. However, the amount
of glucose released into the bloodstream is determined
by the carbohydrate's glycemic index. Any sugar not
absorbed after 30 minutes may be excreted, unused by
the body. The concept of fast- and slow-release
carbohydrates is a myth.

Montignac on carbohydrates

Carbohydrates, also termed sugars, provide the body with its primary source of fuel—glucose. However, eating too many high-GI carbohydrates can lead the pancreas to flood the bloodstream with an excess of glucose, which, in turn, can contribute to weight gain.

TYPES OF CARBOHYDRATES

There are several types of carbohydrates, which are classified according to the complexity of their sugar molecules. Carbohydrates composed of single molecules of sugar are known as monosaccharides. Disaccharides, or carbohydrates containing two molecules of sugar joined together, include sucrose (sugar) and maltose (found in beer). These carbohydrates tend to have high GI values, and they are referred to as simple sugars.

What about starches?

Starches are known as polysaccharides, which are made up of hundreds of glucose and sugar molecules joined together. They are found in bread, grains, legumes, seeds, and in most vegetables. These are known as complex carbohydrates. The GI of a starch is not based strictly on its sugar content, but also on its fiber content (*see box, right*). Refined starches that are low in fiber, such as white bread, have high GI values and are terrible for your weight. Those that are rich in fiber, including green vegetables, have low GI values and can be eaten with a minimal risk of weight gain.

The fast/slow sugar myth

For many years, scientists and nutritionists placed carbohydrates into two distinct categories: "quick sugars" and "slow sugars." These terms referred to the speed at which it was thought the body assimilated the sugars.

"the lower the glycemic index of the carbohydrates you eat, the lower your weight will be."

Simple sugars (monosaccharides and disaccharides) were called "quick sugars." People believed that the simple nature of the molecule meant that these sugars were rapidly assimilated by the body after eating them.

Conversely, complex carbohydrates were called "slow sugars," since they contain a chain of sugar molecules that must first be chemically transformed into simple sugar (glucose) during the course of digestion. This term applied most notably to the starches in whole-grain foods, from which it was thought that glucose was released into the body slowly. This way of classifying carbohydrates is outdated today, since it is based on a mistaken theory.

The new verdict

Recent studies show that the complexity of a carbohydrate's makeup does not determine the speed with which glucose is released into the bloodstream. In other words, the glycemic peak (that is, the point of maximum glucose absorption) is reached at the same rate for any carbohydrate eaten in isolation and on an empty stomach. This occurs about half an hour after ingestion. So, instead of talking about the speed of assimilation, it is more important to consider the effects different carbohydrates have on blood sugar levels—that is, how much glucose they produce in the bloodstream. Therefore, carbohydrates are now classified according to their potential to raise blood sugar levels, as defined by the GI (*see pp18–21*).

Carbohydrates and your weight

The GI of the foods you eat has a direct correlation to your weight and your health. In other words, the lower the glycemic index of the carbohydrates you eat, the lower your weight will be. High-sugar carbohydrates have a GI of above 50. Moderate-GI foods containing a moderate amount of sugar have values between 35 and 50, and low-sugar foods have relatively low GI values of 35 and below.

Refined carbohydrates, such as white bread, have a simpler structure and release more sugar than unrefined carbohydrates such as whole-wheat bread. As a general rule, carbohydrates with simple structures tend to

HIGH-FIBER CARBOHYDRATES

Dietary fiber is a substance found mainly in legumes (such as kidney beans), vegetables, fruit, and whole cereals. Although it has no actual caloric value, fiber plays an important role in the body. Fiber keeps waste products such as fecal matter moving through the digestive tract, thereby preventing constipation. It also reduces the body's absorption of fats and certain toxic food additives, such as artificial colorings. Most importantly, though, fiber has a beneficial effect on obesity. A diet rich in fiber can reduce the levels of glucose absorbed and, subsequently, the amount of insulin released into the bloodstream.

have higher GI values than those with complex structures. This is because the body has to do very little to convert these "simple" carbohydrates into glucose, which raises blood sugar levels.

The body has a more difficult time extracting glucose from complex carbohydrates. As stated earlier, the body has a 30-minute window during which it must absorb the glucose from a food. If it has not done so during this period, the sugar is thought to be simply be excreted from the body, rather than used.

Carbohydrates and weight loss

To lose weight you must exclude carbohydrates with a GI in excess of 35 for most meals. This rules out foods such as white bread, white rice, and potatoes, not to mention sugary colas and other sweets, to keep your insulin response as low as possible. This will not only prevent your body from storing fat, but it will also kick-start the process of breaking down fat stores to provide additional energy for the body, as required. It sounds difficult, but this stringent period is just that—a finite period. For weight maintenance, your choice of carbohydrates is broader, and includes foods with a GI of up to 50.

Carbohydrates and general health

It is important to note that the GI of the carbohydrates you eat not only affects your weight, but can also have an enormous impact on your general health. For example, eating low on the glycemic index may have the added benefit of reducing your total blood cholesterol and triglyceride levels (different forms of fat in the body) if you keep your intake of saturated fats to a minimum as well (*see pp26–31*).

In addition, eliminating high-GI foods can also prevent the onset of type II diabetes, a chronic metabolic disorder. Type II diabetes usually develops over a period of time, and it most commonly affects those who are overweight. Its causes are closely connected to poor glucose tolerance (*see pp14–17*), and it occurs when the body's cells become resistant to insulin secreted by the pancreas. Adhering to this diet plan, however, can help prevent type II diabetes from developing in the first place.

"The countries with the lowest incidence of cardiovascular disease are those that consume olive oil, fruit, legumes, and wine."

Left, opposite: eggplant, zucchini, fennel, and peppers have low GI values and are good carbohydrates.

How the Diet works

This is not a diet in the traditional sense of the word, since it does not restrict the amount of food you can eat over a short period of time. This diet is a balanced way of eating, based on good food choices. Follow the Diet's guidelines on selecting your foods wisely, and you will revitalize your metabolism and shed unwanted weight, permanently.

THE GUIDING PRINCIPLES

There are two main principles that you should remember when following this diet. The first requires you to completely forget about counting calories. The calorific content of food is not important for those who wish to lose weight (*see pp12–13*).

The second guiding principle is that you must choose foods based on their metabolic potential. In other words, choose carbohydrate foods based on the amount of energy, or glucose, that will be absorbed by the body, as expressed by their GI values.

The golden rule

For weight loss, the Diet's golden rule is based on eating as low on the glycemic index as possible. In other words, choose carbohydrates that have low or very low GI values. If your aim is to lose weight quickly, you should choose carbohydrates with a GI value of 35 or below (*see pp104–105*) for most meals. For weight maintenance, or if you choose to lose only a little bit of weight, you may eat carbohydrates with a GI as high as 50, but no higher than this (*see pp152–53*).

For general health, I urge you to choose lean, high-quality proteins. You must also keep your saturated fat intake to a minimum, and choose instead polyunsaturated omega-3 fatty acids (*see pp26–31*), found in fatty fish, such as salmon and mackerel, and monounsaturated fats, such as olive oil and avocados.

"This diet is a balanced way of eating, based on good food choices."

Two plans for two goals

There are two plans in this diet: the Rapid Weight Loss plan (*see pp44–105*) and the Weight Control plan (*see pp106–53*). How rigorous you are in adopting a low-GI way of eating is what distinguishes the two plans from one another.

The Rapid Weight Loss plan is for people who want to lose weight quickly or have a lot of weight to lose. It is naturally a bit more restrictive in terms of the foods you may eat. After you have lost your excess weight and have renormalized your pancreas's response to glucose, you should gradually implement the Weight Control plan over a period of a couple of months for weight maintenance.

If, however, you are more relaxed about how quickly you wish to lose weight or if you do not have a weight problem, you may skip the Rapid Weight Loss plan altogether and go straight to the Weight Control plan. This broader and more permissive eating plan is ideal for those who simply want to eat well, feel terrific, and maintain their current weight.

Where to begin

Before you do anything else, you should set yourself a goal weight. It is important to remember, however, that no two bodies are alike. Some people are more sensitive to glucose than others, and factors such as age, gender, eating habits, and heredity all play a part in determining your weight. These variables make it difficult to determine how much weight you will lose each week.

If you want to lose a lot of weight, I suggest that you begin with the Rapid Weight Loss plan, which can last from several weeks to several months. If you reach your goal weight in a very short period of time, you may be tempted to stop this plan as soon as you have reached your goal weight. I would advise against this. This is because the aim of the Rapid Weight Loss plan is not just to lose weight, but also to stabilize the way your pancreas functions and to raise its tolerance threshold to glucose. This normally takes one to two months. If you cut this plan short prematurely, you may have achieved your goal weight, but you also run the risk of failing to give your pancreas time to become healthy again.

A FRESH START

Perhaps you already have a fairly good idea of how much weight you would like to lose. Many people will be happy to lose 10 pounds (5 kg), even though they really need to shed 20 pounds (10 kg).

Past failures with stop-and-go low-calorie diets may have lowered your expectations. With this diet, however, I would encourage you to be ambitious and set your sights as high as possible.

Good and bad carbohydrates

Since carbohydrates are the only foods that contain sugar, GI values apply only to these foods. Fats and proteins (see pp22–31) contain very little sugar and therefore their impact on blood sugar levels are negligible. For the complete chart of carbohydrates, with precise GI values, see pages 240–45.

Good carbohydrates (GI of 50 and below)	Bad carbohydrates (GI over 50)
Freshly squeezed fruit juice (no added sugar)	Beer
Sweet potatoes	White potatoes (baked, mashed, chips, French fries)
Whole-wheat or rye bread (made from unrefined flour)	White bread
Spaghetti, whole-wheat or durum (cooked al dente)	Ravioli; tortellini; overcooked spaghetti
Unrefined cereals (e.g., large rolled oats)	Refined cereals (e.g., cornflakes)
Wild rice	Semolina
Fructose	Glucose, honey, sugar
Brown rice; unrefined basmati rice	White rice; puffed rice; rice cakes
Carrots (raw)	Carrots (cooked)
Natural yogurt (sugar-free)	Fruit yogurt (sweetened with sugar)
Peas (dried)	Corn (fresh steamed; popcorn)
Quinoa	Couscous
Oat cakes (sugar-free)	Crackers (made from refined flour)
Dried fruit (figs, prunes, apricots)	Raisins, dried bananas, dried coconut
Beans (haricot, French, flageolet)	Risotto rice
Chickpeas (garbanzos)	Tapioca
Flour, unrefined, whole-wheat	Flour, refined, white
Fruit jam and flavored gelatin (sugar-free)	Fruit jam and flavored gelatin (with sugar or grape juice)
Dark chocolate (70 percent cocoa)	Milk chocolate
Cruciferous vegetables	Some starchy vegetables (e.g., parsnips, pumpkin, turnips)
Fresh fruits (excluding bananas, melon, watermelon)	Watermelon, melon, bananas

Good and bad fats

This diet advocates choosing good, low-GI carbohydrates. However, it is also important to eat unsaturated fats and limit your consumption of saturated fats (particularly if you have high cholesterol). The fats below marked with a plus are polyunsaturated, and may reduce total cholesterol.

Good fats (unsaturated)	Bad fats (saturated)
Herring+	Butter
Salmon+	Lard
Tuna+	Beef drippings
Mackerel+	Pork drippings
Sardines+	Lamb drippings
Avocados	Fatty cuts of red meat
Olive oil	Poultry skin
Sunflower oil	Pâté
Sunflower seeds	Hard stick margarine
Walnuts	Hydrogenated oils
Walnut oil	Palm oil
Corn oil	Peanuts
Goose fat	Peanut oil
Macadamia nuts	Coconut
Brazil nuts	Coconut oil
Almonds	Cheese
Flax seeds	Cream
Canola oil	Full-fat milk
Pumpkin seeds	Full-fat sour cream
Pumpkinseed oil	Full-fat yogurt

why it works
digested chapter

_____ **low-calorie diets** can actually slow the rate at which your body burns calories, which will invariably lead to weight gain after the diet has ended.

_____ **excess weight** is the result of an unhealthy pancreas that over-responds to glucose in the bloodstream, producing too much insulin, which leads to glucose being stored as fat instead of burned for energy.

_____ **the glycemic index** is a ranking system that measures the amount of sugar the body will absorb from carbohydrates.

_____ **good carbohydrates** have a GI value of 50 or below. They will not elicit a large insulin response, or cause you to gain weight.

_____ **bad carbohydrates** have GI values above 50. They will trigger a large insulin response, which will contribute to weight gain.

_____ **proteins** are the essential building blocks of life, and they can actually facilitate weight loss. They contain a negligible amount of sugar and they are not measured by the glycemic index.

_____ **good fats** are unsaturated and found in oily fish and vegetable oils. Because they are structurally dissimilar to human fat tissue, they are not easily converted to fatty tissue by the body.

_____ **bad fats** are saturated and found in animal products, such as butter. Avoid bad fats, especially when eating a carbohydrate with a GI higher than 50. This food combination can cause you to gain weight.

_____ **a low–GI diet** will help you to control your weight by suppressing hyperglycemia and hyperinsulinism. The lower you eat on the glycemic index, the more weight you will lose.

RAPID WEIGHT LOSS PLAN

In a nutshell

If your goal is to lose weight quickly and permanently, then the Rapid Weight Loss plan is the right place to start. It will show you how to choose foods that will renormalize your pancreas, boost your metabolism, and trigger fat loss. Before you embark on this plan, however, it is essential that you read all of the preceding pages so that you fully understand the basic principles of the Diet.

THE OBJECTIVES

The aims of the Rapid Weight Loss plan are twofold, but interconnected: first, to facilitate fast, healthful, and sustainable weight loss; second, to calm the way in which your pancreas produces insulin and to reduce its sensitivity to glucose. This, in turn, will improve the efficiency of your metabolism, which will allow you to maintain your weight loss.

Weight loss

If you are used to eating a lot of sugar, or are a dessert fanatic, you will probably experience a dramatic weight loss during your first week on the Rapid Weight Loss plan. This is a normal response, since your body is probably not used to this healthful way of eating. But do not abandon the plan at this point, because in just two days of returning to your old eating habits, you risk regaining the weight it took you a week to lose (*see duration, opposite*). After this initial period, weight loss will occur steadily, but less dramatically than in the first week.

Stabilizing the pancreas

If you are overweight, then it is likely that your pancreas over-responds to bad carbohydrates (such as white bread) by releasing too much insulin in response to the glucose in your bloodstream. At the very least, you will have poor glucose tolerance, and you may even be suffering from

"You may find that you lose your excess weight very quickly."

hyperinsulinism (*see pp14–17*). Both of these conditions are linked to an addiction to high-sugar, high-GI carbohydrates. The amount of insulin your pancreas produces is no longer in the right proportion to the amount of glucose released into your bloodstream after eating a carbohydrate. In short, your pancreas produces too much insulin, which, in turn, leads to weight gain.

Following the rules of the Rapid Weight Loss plan will help you to normalize your pancreas. This will raise your glucose tolerance threshold so that when you do eat a carbohydrate, your body will respond by releasing an appropriate amount of insulin. This will help you to lose weight and keep it off permanently.

The duration

You may find that you lose your excess weight very quickly and, because of this, you may be tempted to cut short the duration of the Rapid Weight Loss plan. You must not succumb to this temptation! Remember, the goal of this plan is not only to lose weight quickly, but to make your pancreas function normally so that you can keep the weight off. No matter what your goal is, you must remain on the Rapid Weight Loss plan for at least a month (and preferably three months) in order to stabilize the metabolic and digestive functions of the body. Sustainable weight loss is not possible without a properly functioning pancreas, and it can take up to three months for this to occur. If you abandon the plan too soon, you may not have given your pancreas sufficient time to recover its equilibrium. If you end the Rapid Weight Loss plan too soon, your success will be short-lived.

What next?

Now that you have familiarized yourself with the foundations of the Diet and the basic objectives of the Rapid Weight Loss plan, you are probably wondering how to get started. The following section will outline the rules of the Rapid Weight Loss plan, which will provide you with everything you need to know about using this eating plan for maximum weight loss. Good luck!

OTHER BENEFITS

If you suffer from hypertriglyceridemia or high cholesterol (*see pp30–31*), this diet should have a therapeutic effect on these levels. Studies have shown that a diet laden with high-GI carbohydrates and saturated fats can contribute to these conditions. This diet restricts the consumption of both of these types of foods, while encouraging the intake of heart-healthy, low-GI carbohydrates and unsaturated fats. This approach has been proven to reduce elevated levels of cholesterol and triglycerides.

rapid weight loss
the rules

1   **never skip a meal,** particularly lunch. Eat until you are full, and remember that counting calories is a useless exercise. Simply follow the basic principles and eat three balanced meals a day at regular intervals.

2   **there are two breakfast** options. Option 1, the carbohydrate-protein breakfast, can include high-fiber bread, but it must be free from saturated fat. Option 2, the protein-fat breakfast, excludes carbohydrates. Because this meal is high in saturated fat, you should only have it twice a week.

3   **there are two types** of lunch and dinner: Option 1, the protein-fat meal, consists of protein and carbohydrates with a GI of 35 and below. Option 2, the high-fiber carbohydrate meal, contains carbohydrates with a GI as high as 50, but the meal must not include any saturated fat at all.

4   **have up to four** high-fiber carbohydrate meals per week. Meals can contain carbohydrates with a GI up to 50, but they must be low in saturated fat.

5 **lunch and dinner** are very similar, but your dinner should be lighter than your lunch. That is, dinner should contain less fat and meat and more low-GI vegetables.

6 **eliminate sugar** in all its forms. This includes not only obvious sugar sources, such as desserts, but also high-GI carbohydrates, and drinks, soups, jams, and other condiments, which can contain hidden sugar.

7 **avoid caffeinated beverages** since caffeine triggers the pancreas to secrete insulin. Avoid coffee, colas, and strong black tea, and drink weak or herbal tea, decaffeinated coffee, and water instead.

8 **limit alcohol consumption** and never drink it on an empty stomach. One 3.5-fl-oz (10-cl) glass of wine or one 3.5-fl-oz (10-cl) glass of beer can be drunk with your lunch and dinner, provided you have eaten a protein-fat snack or some of your meal before taking your first sip.

9 **avoid eating** saturated fats with carbohydrates with a GI above 35. You may have a small amount of monounsaturated fat, such as olive oil, or polyunsaturated fat, found in fatty fish such as salmon. Fish oil will not contribute to weight gain.

Choose foods wisely

Some seemingly healthy foods can actually have dangerously high GI values. This section will examine a few of the big offenders and show you how to choose these caution foods in their least glycemic forms.

- sugar

- starches

- bread

- pasta

- fruit

- drinks

On sugar

Sugar is a colossus in the world of bad carbohydrates. It should come with a health warning, just like cigarettes, for it can be dangerous when consumed in large quantities. With the amounts that are added to most foods, we might be forgiven for thinking sugar is an indispensable ingredient in our diet. Nothing could be farther from the truth!

FRUCTOSE

Compared to ordinary sugar or artificial sweeteners, fructose has definite benefits. To start with, it is a natural sugar and therefore avoids the sorts of problems posed by artificial sweeteners. It also has a low GI of 20, which will have little effect on the pancreas and its production of insulin. Finally, it has a density similar to that of sugar, which means it is useful in baking and cooking. However, it can increase the level of triglycerides (see pp30–31) in some people when used in significant quantities, so people with cholesterol problems should use it in moderation.

THE SUGAR EPIDEMIC

Sugar, by which I mean sucrose, or saccharose, including processed sugars such as white, refined sugar and cane sugar, has a high GI of 70. It is one of the most harmful foods you can put in your body. For tens of thousands of years, man lived quite happily without sugar. The largely indiscriminate use of sugar has evolved in less than 200 years—that is, within the space of five or six generations. It is inconceivable that the human body could adapt fast enough to cope with the perpetually high blood sugar levels associated with such a radical change in diet.

What's more, the situation has deteriorated even further over the last 50 years as other high-GI foods have been added to our diets. As a result, an increasing number of people are finding that their poor pancreases are unprepared for and quite incapable of coping with the heavy demands of a modern high-GI diet. This situation has contributed to the escalating proportion of the population who have found themselves battling with obesity.

What about honey?

Honey is sometimes presented as a healthy and acceptable alternative to sugar, since it is a natural sweetener. However, like sugar, honey has a very high GI value, and it will cause your blood sugar levels to soar; it affects your body in almost exactly the same way as table sugar. In other words, honey is simply another form of sugar to be avoided at all costs.

Hidden sugar

There are two types of sugar: the sugar we recognize, and the sugar we don't. The sugar we recognize is the sugar we add to our food and beverages. We have some degree of control over sugar that we've added ourselves, but the sugar we recognize is only half the problem.

The sugar we don't recognize is a far more sinister beast, since it has been added to our food by others without our knowledge. This is hidden sugar, widely used by the food companies and pharmaceuticals industries to give their products bulk and render them palatable for mass consumption. This means that even seemingly benign substances, such as cough syrups and cough drops, often contain sugar of some kind.

Take a look at almost any food packaging label and you will be amazed at how many commercially prepared foods contain sugar. These hidden sugars can be found under many different names, including sucrose, dextrose, malt, corn syrup, molasses, and honey. Fortunately, nutrition labels now tell you how many grams of sugar are contained in one serving of a food, so be vigilant when it comes to reading labels, and take nothing for granted.

Maintaining blood sugar

Some may ask, if we eliminate sugar from our diet completely, how will we be able to maintain minimum sugar levels in our blood? That is a good question, and the answer is simple. As I pointed out in Chapter One, the body needs glucose, not sugar, for energy. Fruit, whole foods, legumes, and particularly cereals can easily provide the body with all the glucose it needs under normal circumstances. And if there is a temporary lack of carbohydrates to keep the body going (as may happen when the body is engaged in strenuous physical activity), the body is quite capable of drawing on other energy reserves, such as stored fat. So there is no need to eat sugar.

Initially, this may cause problems for people who like to sweeten their food. In which case, I recommend using an artificial sweetener (*see box, right*), such as saccharin, sucralose, or aspartame, temporarily until their palates become accustomed to their new regimen.

ARTIFICIAL SWEETENERS

Although using artificial sweeteners temporarily can help to wean you off sugar, prolonged use could disturb your metabolism in the long term. This is because the body detects sweetness and prepares itself to digest carbohydrates, which then fail to materialize.

Therefore, if you consume a large amount of artificial sweetener during the course of the day, any consumption of genuine carbohydrates in the next 24 hours may result in an excessive spike in your blood sugar level, which is then followed by a hypoglycemic reaction.

Artificial sweeteners exacerbate the hypo- and hyperglycemia cycle (*see p15*), which, in turn, contributes to intense feelings of hunger and the accumulation of body fat. In short, artificial sweeteners can indirectly contribute to weight gain.

On starches

Starches are complex carbohydrates. Some of them, such as lentils and other legumes, have low GI values and are therefore considered good carbohydrates. However, many starches, including potatoes, white rice, and corn, are bad carbohydrates with high GI values. Eating these starches will prevent you from normalizing your pancreas and losing weight.

THE POTATO

The number one bad starchy food on this diet is the potato. When the potato was brought back from the New World in 1540, the French declined to eat the tuber and gave it to their pigs instead. For two centuries, the French continued to scoff at what they called "the pig tuber." It was not until 1789, when famine raged through the country, that the French finally started to eat potatoes.

Why is it unhealthy?

When raw, the potato is undoubtedly a good food, since it is rich in vitamins and minerals. Unfortunately, it also contains starches that humans are unable to digest. Humans simply lack the necessary enzymes with which pigs are blessed. In order to make potatoes digestible, we must cook them. And although this makes the potato more digestible, it also breaks down its starches, raising its GI value and making it less suitable for our metabolism.

Recent experiments have shown that the potato releases a large amount of glucose when it is digested because of the poor quality of its fiber. When peeled and boiled, a potato has a GI of about 70. Processing the potato (as in instant mashed potatoes) raises the GI to about 80. Fried potatoes, French fries, and potato chips have a GI of 95, and they cannot be ingested without the risk of gaining weight, since the oil used for frying can be laid down as fat reserves.

"When the potato was brought back from the New World, the French declined to eat the tuber and gave it to their pigs instead."

CARROTS

Like potatoes, the starch in carrots is radically affected by heat and the cooking process. Luckily, raw carrots have a low GI of 30, and, unlike raw potatoes, they are digestible by humans. Raw carrots can therefore be eaten freely on the Rapid Weight Loss plan.

Raw carrots are delicious grated as a side salad, dressed in a vinaigrette. For extra flavor, briefly dry-roast some mustard seeds and sprinkle them over the carrots.

A carrot only becomes a bad carbohydrate when it is cooked.

Boiling, baking, steaming, or grilling a carrot breaks down its starches, causing the GI to rise dramatically to about 85. Predictably, this makes cooked carrots an unacceptable carbohydrate choice on the Rapid Weight Loss plan.

However, carrots, raw or cooked, have a low concentration of carbohydrates (*see pp114–15*), which means that on the Weight Control Plan (*see pp106–53*), you can reintroduce cooked carrots into your diet, in moderation.

"White rice, in the form in which it is eaten in the West, is a highly processed food and a dietary disaster waiting to happen."

On the other hand, when it is boiled in its skin, the GI of a potato can be as low as 65 (although this is still high). Potatoes were usually cooked and eaten this way in the past, together with high-fiber vegetables, which helped to lower the total GI (*see pp112–14*) of the dish, by adding fiber.

So if you want to lose weight on the Rapid Weight Loss plan, you must avoid potatoes. Forgoing potatoes may be a major sacrifice, but it is worth the price to achieve your goal of a slim and healthy body. Once that goal is achieved, however, I promise you will have no regrets. If you must have a potato, have a sweet potato instead, since it has a lower GI of 50. On the Rapid Weight Loss plan, sweet potatoes are acceptable as part of a high-fiber carbohydrate meal, but eat them in the old-fashioned way—boiled or baked with the skin on and served with low-GI vegetables, such as string beans, spinach, cauliflower, or even a salad.

CORN

Corn is another starchy food that is popular in the Western world. It was grown for thousands of years by the native populations of the Americas as part of their staple diet. Still preserved in agricultural museums, the ancient varieties of Indian corn were rich in soluble fiber and had a GI of 35. With the discovery of the new world, Westerners set about growing corn for themselves, and particularly for their livestock. Today's form of corn, however, has a very high GI value and should therefore be avoided on the Diet.

Why is it unhealthy?

To increase the amount of corn they could grow, farmers and scientists began a process of selection and hybridization. Within a few decades, the genetic modification of corn caused its GI to almost double, to around 65. The starch in today's corn is now so fragile that when it is processed and changed into cornflakes or popcorn, its GI jumps from 65 to 85.

In addition, over-irrigation of modern corn has depleted it of much of its former nutritional content. So, unfortunately, the corn that is available to us today is not the same as it was 500 years ago. It is low in fiber, vitamins, and minerals, but high in bad starch.

As a result, the corn available today causes the pancreas to release a large amount of glucose as it is digested. This, in turn, triggers the pancreas to produce huge amounts of insulin, which can cause pancreatic sensitivity and weight gain. Since they have very high GI values, corn and all corn products, including popcorn and cornflakes, should be omitted from your meals and snacks throughout the Diet.

RICE AND OTHER GRAINS

White rice, in the form in which it is eaten in the West, is a highly processed food and a dietary disaster waiting to happen. It is high in bad starch and very low in fiber and other nutrients. Processing rice, or overcooking it, will raise its GI value even more, and the more glutinous, or sticky, the rice becomes, the higher its GI. For example, parboiled rice, or instant rice, has a GI of about 90. Processed products such as rice cakes and puffed rice cakes also have high GI values of roughly 85.

Why is it unhealthy?

White rice is refined to the point that nothing remains of nutritive value except the one thing we could happily do without: starch. Predictably, it is a bad carbohydrate that releases large amounts of glucose into the bloodstream. Ordinary, refined white rice has a very high GI value and should be therefore completely eliminated from the Rapid Weight Loss plan in the Diet.

Conversely, the types of rice eaten in non-Western countries, such as unrefined basmati and long-grain brown rice, have not been stripped of their fibrous husk, which is a key element in reducing a food's GI value. Therefore, basmati and long-grain brown rice have a medium GI of about 50 and may be eaten as part of your high-fiber carbohydrate lunches and dinners on the Rapid Weight Loss plan, and whenever you wish on the Weight Control plan.

You can also have wild rice (*see right*), which has a very low GI, any time you want. Whatever you do, though, avoid eating refined white rice, puffed rice, and rice cakes at all costs. These high-GI foods will invariably lead to weight gain.

WILD RICE

There are no restrictions on eating wild rice on the Diet. Wild rice has a delicious nutty flavor and a low GI value of 35, and you may therefore eat it freely. A little-known fact is that it is in fact an oat, and not a rice at all. Another low-GI carbohydrate to be enjoyed without restrictions is quinoa, a protein-rich, grainlike seed, which also has a low GI of 35.

RIZ CAMARGUE *LOTOS-complet ou CULTURE SICILE*

LENTILLES Corail *VALS*

SOJA vert *...*

Riz pré-cuit

HAMZA Semoule grosse Complement

RIZ Complet *16.*

COUSCOUS - TABOULÉ *...de blé*

RIZ CAMARGUE
de culture biologique

BOULGHOUR
pil-pil
blé concassé *GROS*

celnat

BOULLHOUR
pil-pil
blé concassé *FIN*

BEANS AND LEGUMES

You might expect me to condemn beans and legumes, given what we know about the potato (*see pp54–56*). Well, you are mistaken! Most legumes, including chickpeas (garbanzos), haricot beans, French beans, and split peas, have very low GI values of 35 and below. Lentils have one of the lowest GIs of all legumes. Green lentils, for instance, have a GI of 25. Also included here are the distinctive Puy lentils.

These legumes are high in fiber and have very low GI values. They can therefore facilitate weight loss, and are categorized as good carbohydrates. They can be eaten freely at any meal, but without any fat such as butter or lard on the Rapid Weight Loss plan. Although kidney beans have a slightly higher GI value of 35, they also may be included as a part of any meal on the Rapid Weight Loss plan.

rapid weight loss
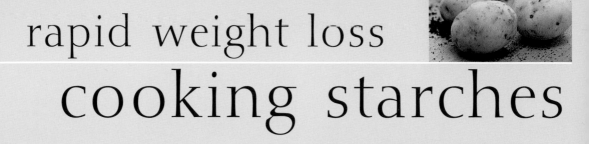
cooking starches

when a potato is peeled and boiled, the GI increases from 65 to 70. When potatoes are processed into instant mashed potatoes, their GI rises by as much as 15 points, from 65 to 80.

potato chips or French fries have a GI value as high as 95, and they cannot be ingested without the risk of gaining weight. This is because the oil used for frying can be laid down as fat reserves.

overcooking rice raises its GI value. The more glutinous, or sticky, the rice is, the higher its GI will be. Precooked rice has a very high GI of 90. Processing rice to make products such as rice cakes and puffed rice gives these foods a high GI value of 85.

—————————— **overcooking pasta** will increase its GI value. The longer it cooks in the pot, the higher the GI will rise, since more of its starch will gelatinize and become digestible.

———— **cooking pasta *al dente*** keeps its GI as low as possible. Eating pasta cold will cause its GI to go down by a further five points through a cooling process known as retrogradation.

—————————— **cooking carrots** causes their GI value to rise sharply from 30 to 85, which makes this otherwise good carbohydrate a bad one.

———— **toasting bread** may bring down the GI of a piece of bread by several points through a process known as retrogression.

—————————— **when corn** is heated to produce popcorn, or processed to make cornflakes, its GI increases appreciably, jumping from 65 to 85.

Q&A

Can I eat bread?

Bread could easily have been the subject of a whole chapter. When eaten in moderation, "good" bread, which is rich in fiber, is not fattening. Unfortunately, these days it is a rare commodity. There is plenty of bread around, of course, but most of it is a parody of the real thing, and therefore potentially fattening.

Q How can bread be fattening?

Some breads (but not all) have GI values as high as sugar. Predictably, because your pancreas does not differentiate between foods, it will react to bread or sugar in exactly the same way—that is, by releasing a large amount of insulin to bring down blood sugar levels. And, as you know, it is this surge in insulin that gives rise to fat storage and weight gain.

Q What kind of bread should I avoid?

White bread, which is made from refined flour, is almost totally devoid of all those elements necessary to feed a healthy metabolism, such as fiber, vitamins, and minerals. Nutritionally, its only contribution to the body is energy in the form of starch. From the digestive point of view, it can only give rise to problems, since it lacks the fiber necessary for good digestion. It is worth remembering that the whiter the bread, the more it should be considered a bad carbohydrate, since the degree of whiteness indicates the amount of refining that has taken place.

Q What kind of bread can I eat?

High-fiber breads, such as rye, whole-wheat bread, or bread made with unrefined organic flour, have the lowest GI values, which range from 40 to 50. Their relatively low GI values have little impact on blood sugar levels, and so are less "fattening" than refined white bread. As a general rule, the softer and squishier the bread, the higher its GI will probably be.

Q When can I eat bread?

Bread (even good varieties) should only be eaten for breakfast, as part of the carbohydrate-protein breakfast option. This is because even good bread is high in starch, and has a GI value higher than 35. When you start applying the Diet's principles, you must be wary of increasing the overall GI of your meal more than necessary in order to keep the level of insulin in your body as low as possible.

"There is plenty of bread around, but most of it is a parody of the real thing."

Q&A

Can I eat pasta?

You probably expect me to tell you that pasta should be omitted from your diet. Well, just to surprise you, I will do the opposite and say not all pasta is bad. While some pastas have high GI values and should be avoided, other kinds, when cooked in the right way, have relatively low GI values. They can even facilitate weight loss, and are therefore acceptable on the Rapid Weight Loss plan.

Q Can I eat pasta?

Yes, but the type of wheat used to make your pasta does matter. If you want to eat white pasta, it should always be a pastified variety (*see opposite*) made from durum wheat, not soft wheat. Durum-wheat pasta contains more protein and fiber than soft-wheat varieties, and this lowers its GI value. If you are not sure what type of wheat has been used, it's best to avoid white pasta, and eat whole-wheat pasta instead. Whole-wheat pasta has a higher fiber content than white pasta, which gives it a low GI of 40. Although it is five points higher than the recommended GI of 35, you may eat whole-wheat pasta in moderation on the Rapid Weight Loss plan.

Q When and how often can I eat it?

While following the Rapid Weight Loss plan, you can eat the recommended types of pasta (*see above*) up to four times per week as part of your three to four high-fiber carbohydrate meals. You should space these meals out over the course of a week; for example, don't have pasta for lunch and dinner on the same day.

Q What is pastification?

Pastification is a mechanical process in which pasta dough is fed through small holes at a very high pressure. This gives the pasta a protective film, which limits the amount of starch gelatinization that can take place during the cooking process. This film lowers the pasta's GI value by about five points, thereby limiting the amount of glucose released into the bloodstream. The most common pastified pastas are spaghetti, linguini, and vermicelli.

Q Does it matter how I cook it?

Whatever pasta you choose, cook it *al dente*, or as firm as possible, since overcooking pasta makes more of its starch digestible, which will increase its GI value. If you accidentally overcook your pasta, you can limit the damage by eating it cold, because the GI goes down through retrogradation, or the cooling process. So, always choose pastified pastas (spaghetti is best) made from a high-fiber flour, and eat it *al dente*.

Q Which pasta has the lowest GI?

Chinese vermicelli, which is really more of a noodle than a pasta, is a different ballgame altogether, even though it was the original inspiration for spaghetti. It is different because Chinese vermicelli is made not from wheat flour, like most pastas, but from soy flour. This gives it a very low GI of 22. Since it is also pastified, you can eat as much Chinese vermicelli as you like on the Diet. This means that you can include Chinese vermicelli in any of your main meals, regardless of whether they are protein-fat meals or high-fiber carbohydrate meals.

"Chinese vermicelli is a different ballgame altogether."

On fruit

Fruit is often a contentious issue when it comes to diets, and were I so foolish as to suggest that you should exclude fruit from your diet, a large number of you would shut the book at this point and read no further. So I will reassure you right away: the Diet will not exclude fruit at any point. In most cultures, fruit is a symbol associated with life, health, and vitality—and for good reason. Most fruits are not only delicious, but also good for you.

FRUIT AND GI

Fruit contains carbohydrates, such as glucose, sucrose, and, above all, fructose. This means that it is important to be vigilant about the GI values of fruit. While it's hard to actually gain weight from eating fruit, to trigger fat loss, you must limit your fruit selection to those that have a GI of 35 or below on the Rapid Weight Loss plan. Luckily, fruit also contains a soluble fiber known as pectin, which lowers the GI by reducing the amount of sugar absorbed by the body.

To peel or not to peel?

Since much of the fiber of a fruit is contained in the skin, peeled fruits tend to have higher GI values than those that are eaten with the skin on. In addition, it is there, close to the surface, that you will find the greatest concentration of vitamins. It is therefore very important to eat the whole fruit, including the skin, in order to keep the GI low and thus help you lose weight more easily.

Fruit won't make you fat

The muscles in the body can easily use the energy available from fruit. Fruit sugar is converted to glycogen and stored in the muscles rather being turned into body fat. This is why some dried fruits, such as dried

"To trigger fat loss, you must limit your fruit selection to those that have a GI of 35 or below."

figs, can also be considered good, high-fiber fruit options, despite the fact that they have a GI of 40. Some of the best fruit options for Rapid Weight Loss, however, include apples and prunes, which are both high in pectin and have an acceptably low GI value of below 35. (*For more fruit options on the Rapid Weight Loss plan, see pp68–69.*)

That said, it is best to avoid high-GI fruits, such as bananas, raisins, kiwi fruit, watermelon, melon, and grapes while on the Rapid Weight Loss plan. Their GI values greatly exceed 35, and they may prevent you from losing weight.

Fruit juices

With the exception of lemon juice, which is very low in sugar, it is best to exclude fruit juice from your diet on the Rapid Weight Loss plan and eat fresh fruit instead. Freshly squeezed fruit juice passes through the body quickly, just as fresh fruit does. However, fruit juice has a higher GI value than whole fruit, since the juicing process strips it of most of its fiber.

Commercial fruit juices, even those labeled "pure fruit," with no added sugar, should be consumed even less often than freshly squeezed juices. Their vitamin and fiber content is lower than that of freshly squeezed fruit, and they normally contain high levels of acid, which is bad for digestion.

Fruit and indigestion

If, like a small percentage of the population, you suffer from digestive problems, you should eat fresh fruit on an empty stomach only. Contrary to what many believe, this has nothing to do with weight loss, but rather helps ease digestion. To be sure your stomach is truly empty, you should only consume fruit three hours after a meal, or at least 20 minutes before a meal.

For some people, eating fruit during or directly after a meal may cause bloating indigestion, since the fruit can get "trapped" in the stomach, where the heat and humidity cause it to ferment. Luckily, this does not apply to all fruits and there are some exceptions to the rule (*see right*). If you do not suffer from digestive problems, feel free to eat any fresh fruit with a GI value of 35 or below with your meal, or directly following it.

FRIENDLY FRUITS

If you are prone to indigestion (*see left, below*), it is best to eat fruit on an empty stomach. However, every rule has its exception, and there are some fruits that will not cause indigestion. Strawberries, raspberries, blackberries, red currants, lemons, and bilberries can all be eaten during or directly after your meal. They contain so little sugar that they are unlikely to ferment in the gut and cause indigestion. Cooked fruits can be eaten, too, because the cooking process deactivates the enzymes that cause fruits to ferment.

WHAT CAN I EAT?

Apples (*right*) are one of the best fruits to choose on the Rapid Weight Loss plan. They are high in vitamins and fiber and have a very low GI. Have them with your breakfast, or on their own for dessert or a snack.

Other fruits that are acceptable for the Rapid Weight Loss plan include:

- **blackberries**
- **cherries**
- **dried apples**
- **dried apricots**
- **dried figs**
- **fresh apricots**
- **fresh figs**
- **grapefruit**
- **oranges**
- **peaches**
- **pears**
- **plums**
- **prunes**
- **raspberries**
- **strawberries**

On drinks

What you drink is almost as important as what you eat. Avoid beverages such as carbonated drinks, fruit juice, coffee, strong black tea, and full-fat milk, since they all contain ingredients that may sabotage your new eating regimen. Instead, retrain your palette to appreciate the more delicate flavors of still or sparkling mineral water with a twist of fresh lemon or lime.

TEA

Strong black tea can be as bad for your waistline as coffee (*see right, below*), since it also contains a lot of caffeine. A better choice would be herbal or fruit teas, such as peppermint or lemon. They are almost always naturally decaffeinated, or contain negligible amounts of caffeine. However, for those of you who cannot imagine life without black tea, weak tea can be a good, low-caffeine compromise.

MILK

Full-fat milk is a complex food, consisting of proteins, carbohydrates (lactose, or milk sugars), and saturated fats. This combination of protein, milk sugar, and saturated fat (*see pp28–29*) may encourage weight gain by trapping the saturated fat in the body as fatty tissue.

It is therefore preferable to drink skim milk or, if you wish, powdered skim milk; you can also add skim milk to your tea and coffee. I find that if you use more powdered milk than is recommended, you can produce a thick, smooth liquid that is rich in proteins and can help you to lose weight. (*For more on milk, see pp126–27.*)

COFFEE

Avoid American-style infused coffee, which is made with boiling water and then filtered. It is a wolf in sheep's clothing, since, although it seems light and mild, it contains a lot of caffeine—more than strong espresso. Although coffee is not a carbohydrate, the caffeine it contains stimulates the pancreas to secrete a small amount of insulin. This is why I would advise excluding regular coffee from your regimen on the Rapid Weight Loss plan, and replace it with decaffeinated coffee or herbal tea.

If you feel you cannot completely eliminate coffee with caffeine from your diet, you can drink 100 percent arabica coffee. This type of coffee may contain less caffeine than the robusta coffee typically sold in cans at the supermarket, and will therefore have less impact on your pancreas.

CARBONATED DRINKS

Choose sparkling mineral water with a twist of lemon or lime over colas and other soft drinks. Carbonated soft drinks are usually based on synthetic fruit and plant extracts and have two major flaws: they contain too much sugar and too much caffeine.

Even sugar-free soft drinks can cause an increase in blood sugar levels, since they contain caffeine and artificial sweeteners such as aspartame, both of which trick the pancreas into thinking it is getting sugar (*see pp52–53*).

Carbonated soft drinks also contain artificial gases that give rise to gas and bloating. The worst offenders among these types of drinks are colas, but artificially flavored fruit drinks are nearly as bad. In short, they should be excluded from your diet completely.

Can I drink alcohol?

From wine to beer to champagne, alcohol plays an important part in our lives, but when drunk to excess, it can lead to weight gain. The Diet will show you how to indulge in your favorite beverages without disrupting your metabolism and gaining weight. As long as your consumption of these drinks is reasonable, they should have no effect on your waistline.

Q How does alcohol cause weight gain?

You should not drink alcohol before a meal. If you do, you will not lose weight. This is because alcohol provides energy that is easily used by the body. When you drink alcohol on an empty stomach, the body does not use its fat reserves as a source of energy—it uses the alcohol instead. In this way, alcohol prevents the body from losing weight. But this happens only when the stomach is empty. The presence of food in the stomach prevents the alcohol from being immediately released into the bloodstream and speeding up the fat storage process.

Q What should I eat before drinking?

When the stomach is already full, particularly with fats and proteins in the form of meat, fish, and cheese, alcohol is metabolized far less rapidly. Two or three cubes of cheese and a slice of dried sausage, all about the size of dice, will be sufficient to line the stomach and slow down the rate at which alcohol is absorbed into the bloodstream, thereby preventing a spike in blood sugar levels.

Q Can I drink wine and champagne?

Yes. One 3.5-fl-oz (10-cl) glass of wine or champagne, drunk toward the end of your main meals, will have no adverse effect. Red wine is preferable to white wine since it is rich in antioxidants (*see pp130–31*). Your wine, whether red or white, should be dry and free from additives and preservatives. If these conditions cannot be met, then it is best to drink organic wine or refrain from drinking wine altogether on the Rapid Weight Loss plan. These drinks won't trigger any insulin response, so you can have up to two small glasses per day on the Rapid Weight Loss plan. However, you must always eat a small protein-fat snack before taking your first sip.

Q Can I drink apéritifs?

No! Apéritifs must be avoided on this plan. By definition, these are drinks consumed before eating, and this can wreak havoc on your metabolism. Spirits, such as vodka, gin, and whiskey, have a very high alcohol content, which will disrupt the metabolism, preventing weight loss and contributing to weight gain. Whenever possible, have a nonalcoholic beverage, such as tomato juice, instead.

Q What about beer?

Beer should be drunk in great moderation, since it contains not only alcohol, but also maltose, a carbohydrate with a very high GI of 110. When beer is drunk between meals, or without eating a protein-fat snack first, it causes weight gain, particularly around the abdomen. If you cannot bear to abstain from drinking beer, you can consume one 3.5-fl-oz (10-cl) glass toward the end of each main meal (i.e., lunch and dinner) each day. That said, your attempts at losing weight will be far more successful if you can totally abstain from drinking beer on the Rapid Weight Loss plan.

rapid weight loss
digested chapter

renormalize the way your pancreas responds to glucose in the bloodstream, and this will help you to lose weight. You must stay on this plan for at least three months, even if you lose weight rapidly.

avoid sugar in all its forms. Get in the habit of reading labels, since many seemingly innocuous foods contain hidden sugar.

choose good starches that have a GI of 50 or below. These foods include raw carrots, brown rice, unrefined basmati rice, wild rice, spaghetti, quinoa, and most legumes, particularly lentils and chickpeas.

avoid bad starches that have a GI over 50. These include white potatoes, white bread, corn, and white refined rice.

_____ **cooking can increase** the GI of some carbohydrates by breaking down molecular bonds, which makes more starch digestible. Most notably, this affects carrots, rice, pasta, and potatoes.

_____ **eat good bread** for breakfast at least five days per week as part of the carbohydrate-protein option. Always choose high-fiber, whole-wheat, or rye bread, and never eat it with saturated fats.

_____ **eat spaghetti,** but always cook it _al dente_. Pastified pastas, such as spaghetti, made from durum-wheat or whole-wheat flour have an acceptably low GI value of 40 (or 35 when allowed to cool).

_____ **avoid caffeinated** drinks, such as coffee, strong tea, and soft drinks, since caffeine stimulates the pancreas to produce insulin.

_____ **limit your alcohol** intake to no more than two 3.5-fl oz (10-cl) glasses of wine, or 7 fl oz (20 cl) of beer, per day. Never drink alcohol on an empty stomach.

RAPID WEIGHT LOSS: MEAL OPTIONS

Breakfast the Montignac way

There are two types of breakfast you can enjoy on the Diet. Option 1 is a carbohydrate-protein meal (*see pp80–81*) and Option 2 is a protein-fat meal (*see pp82–83*). The first option is rich in low-GI carbohydrates, and it is the type of breakfast you should have most often—at least five days per week. The second, called the protein-fat option, is high in both protein and fat, and low in carbohydrates. Since it contains saturated fats, this breakfast is less healthy than Option 1, and should be eaten no more than twice per week.

Option 1
carbohydrate-protein breakfast

This breakfast option is a staple meal on the Diet and should be eaten on most mornings (at least five times per week). It consists of little or no fat, a low-fat or fat-free protein, and a low-GI carbohydrate. This meal is unique on this plan in that it allows you to have bread. In fact, you can eat as much whole-wheat bread as you like with this breakfast, as long as the rest of the breakfast does not contain any fat.

CARBOHYDRATE ELEMENT

The low-GI carbohydrate food is an integral part of this breakfast. You could choose whole-wheat or rye toast, since these breads have moderately low GI values. On the Rapid Weight Loss plan, the only time bread is acceptable is in the morning because your blood sugar level is low when you wake up, and your body is unlikely to produce an excess of glucose in response to the bread.

Other carbohydrate options include sugar-free oat cakes or sugar-free whole-grain cereal, such as jumbo organic oat flakes, mixed cereal flakes, or sugar-free muesli. Corn- or rice-based cereals should be avoided, since they have high GI values. Eat as much as you like, but make sure that your carbohydrate is rich in fiber and contains no added fat or sugar.

PROTEIN ELEMENT

The protein element of your breakfast must be very low in saturated fat. Fat-free, plain natural yogurt is an ideal protein component, since it is rich in protein, free from fats, and low in carbohydrates. Skim milk and fat-free cottage cheese are also good protein options. If you like, you can mix some sugar-free fruit jam with your yogurt or cottage cheese, or alternatively, you can spread it on your toast or oat cakes.

WHAT CAN I EAT?

The breakfast on the left is a well-balanced carbohydrate-protein breakfast, which includes whole-wheat toast spread with sugar-free jam, low-fat natural yogurt with berries, and a cup of decaffeinated coffee. To create a different breakfast, try combining any of the following elements.

For your carbohydrate element, choose from the following:
- rye bread
- bread made with unrefined organic flour
- sugar-free oat cakes
- sugar-free whole-grain cereal

For your protein element, choose from the following:
- fat-free cheese
- fat-free cottage cheese
- fat-free natural yogurt
- skim milk

To drink, choose one of the following:
- decaffeinated coffee
- pure arabica coffee
- herbal or fruit tea

Extras can include:
- sugar-free jam or jelly
- fruits with a sub-35 GI value
- fructose or an artificial sweetener

Option 2
protein-fat breakfast

Option 2 is a good breakfast for when good carbohydrates, such as whole-wheat bread, are unavailable. It contains protein and saturated fat, and it excludes carbohydrates with a GI above 35. This is because these carbohydrates will stimulate the pancreas to produce insulin, which will trap the meal's fat in the body as stored fat. Because of its high saturated fat content, this meal should be eaten no more than twice a week.

PROTEIN ELEMENT

This meal should consist of protein in the form of ham, fish, cheese, or eggs any style. A typical example of this breakfast might be an omelet made with Gruyère cheese, served with fried lardons (*see right*). It is essential, however, that this meal be completely free from carbohydrates with a GI above 35. This ensures that insulin levels in the blood are kept to a minimum, so that the body will not store the fat you've just eaten. In other words, you should never eat bread, toast, or cereal with this breakfast option, but very low-GI vegetables are fine.

FAT ELEMENT

You can prepare this meal using oil or butter and add flavor to your breakfast in the form of fat, such as bacon. These foods are high in saturated fat, and are therefore categorized as the fat component of your breakfast. It is worth mentioning that many of the recommended Option 2 foods are considered complex foods, meaning some of the foods categorized as fat elements contain protein, while some of the protein elements contain fat. Regardless, you may eat as much as you like of any of these foods, so long as your breakfast does not contain carbohydrates with a GI above 35. Balance this meal by selecting foods for lunch and dinner that are high in low-GI carbohydrates and low in saturated fats.

WHAT CAN I EAT?

The breakfast to the left is a good example of the protein-fat meal. It includes an omelet made with Gruyère cheese, served with fried lardons and a cup of decaffeinated coffee. To create a completely different protein-fat breakfast, try combining any of the following elements.

For your protein element, choose from the following:
- eggs, any style
- fish, including smoked salmon
- meat such as ham
- poultry, such as turkey or chicken

For your fat element, choose from the following:
- bacon
- cheese
- lardons
- sausage

To drink, choose from the following:
- decaffeinated coffee
- pure arabica coffee
- herbal or fruit tea

Lunch the Montignac way

Lunch is treated in much the same way as breakfast on the Diet. That is, there are two flexible lunch options to choose from. Option 1 is a protein-fat meal, and this should be your staple lunch. It consists of protein-rich foods such as fish, meat, eggs, or poultry and carbohydrates with a GI no higher than 35. Option 2 is a high-fiber carbohydrate meal, composed of high-fiber, low- to medium-GI carbohydrates with a GI up to 50. This second type of meal should be limited to three to four times per week, and should never be eaten with saturated fats.

Option 1
protein-fat lunch

The Option 1 lunch is a staple meal on the Rapid Weight Loss plan. It may consist of a soup, salad, and side dish made from carbohydrates with a GI of 35 or below, and protein, such as meat, poultry, eggs, or fish. These elements make it an ideal option for weight loss. Its success for slimming, however, hinges on eating only sub-35 GI carbohydrates.

SOUPS, APPETIZERS, AND SALADS

Start your meal with a soup made from vegetables with a very low GI value of 35 or below. Homemade soups such as gazpacho or mushroom soup are best, since commercially prepared soups may contain hidden sugars in the form of corn starch and corn meal.

Other appetizers can be made up of a selection of vegetables with a sub-35 GI value. Feel free to use fats such as oil or butter when preparing this dish. For example, zucchini sautéed in olive oil would make an ideal appetizer for this type of meal. You can also have a side salad prepared with olive oil and cheese, such as leek and asparagus salad (*see pp166–67*). It's perfectly acceptable for these dishes to contain fat, as long as they do not include carbohydrates with a GI higher than 35.

MAIN COURSE

A dish containing a protein source, such as meat, fish, chicken, or eggs, should be the main course in this type of meal. There are no restrictions on the type or amount of protein you choose, but they should always be prepared without bad carbohydrates, such as bread crumbs or flour. If you have high cholesterol, however, it is best to choose protein with a lower fat content, such as tofu, fish, skinless chicken, or lean pork. You can finish off your meal with a small glass of wine or beer and some cheese for dessert (*for more Rapid Weight Loss dessert options, see pp90–91*).

WHAT CAN I EAT?

The lunch to the left is a well-balanced protein-fat meal, consisting of roasted tomatoes and zucchini, which are low-GI carbohydrates, and lean grilled duck with a black olive tapenade, which fulfills the protein and fat requirements. Feel free to choose from the selection of foods below to create your ideal protein-fat meal. Remember, you can prepare these foods with fat, if you wish.

For your sub-35 GI carbohydrate element, choose from the following:
- low-GI vegetables, such as broccoli, peppers, and spinach
- low-GI legumes and grains, such as lentils, quinoa, or wild rice

For your protein element, choose from the following:
- meat
- fish
- poultry
- eggs
- soy products such as tofu

To drink, you can choose one of the following:
- still or sparkling water
- one 3.5-fl-oz (10-cl) glass of wine or champagne
- one 3.5-fl-oz (10-cl) glass of beer

Option 2
high-fiber carbohydrate lunch

This carbohydrate meal should contain minimal, if any, fat, and it should be eaten no more than 3 to 4 times per week. Like Option 1, it can include a soup, salad, and side dish made from very low-GI vegetables. For your main course, however, you can consume carbohydrates with a GI as high as 50.

SOUPS, APPETIZERS, AND SALADS

A broth-based soup made from vegetables with a sub-35 GI value is a great way to start this meal. If you use a canned soup, be vigilant and always scan the label to make sure it contains no hidden sugar or fat.

Your appetizer can include a selection of chopped or steamed vegetables with a sub-35 GI value. You should not add any saturated fats, such as butter, when preparing this dish. Steamed artichokes, for example, would make a filling and healthy side dish or appetizer for this meal. You can also have a salad prepared with a dressing made from fat-free yogurt, mustard, and lemon juice. Alternatively, you may drizzle a tiny bit of olive oil mixed with lemon juice or balsamic vinegar on your salad.

MAIN COURSE

Your main dish should be a high-fiber, sub-50-GI carbohydrate, so long as it is not bread (not even good, whole-wheat bread). You might choose legumes, such as lentils, chickpeas, or haricot beans, brown or unrefined basmati rice, or whole-wheat spaghetti cooked *al dente*. Try some lentils cooked with onions and topped with fat-free natural yogurt or a bowl of whole-wheat spaghetti cooked *al dente*, drizzled with a little olive oil (*see right*). The fat you use should be minimal, and it should always be unsaturated. This means that this should be a meat-free meal. You may also have a small glass of wine or beer with your meal, followed by a low-fat dessert (*for more Rapid Weight Loss dessert options, see pp90–91*).

CAN I JUST EAT PASTA?

Unfortunately, no. This type of meal must include a range of very low-GI vegetables in addition to pasta or any other medium-GI, high-fiber carbohydrate. Colorful vegetables, such as salad greens and tomatoes, provide your body with essential vitamins and minerals, and their very low GI values will help to bring down the total GI of your meal via the AGI principle (*see pp112–14*). So, enjoy your pasta or brown rice, and eat as much as you like, but whatever you do, don't forget to eat your vegetables!

WHAT CAN I EAT?

The lunch to the left is a good example of a high-fiber carbohydrate meal. It includes whole-wheat spaghetti (served cold) with herbs and vegetables, served with a side salad. Feel free to choose from the selection of foods below to create your ideal high-fiber carbohydrate meal. This meal should be prepared with very little fat; avoid saturated fat altogether.

For your sub-35 GI carbohydrate element, choose from the following:
- low-GI vegetables, such as broccoli, peppers, and spinach
- low-GI legumes and grains, such as lentils, quinoa, and wild rice

For your high-fiber carbohydrate element, choose from the following:
- whole-wheat spaghetti (preferably served cold to reduce its GI value)
- legumes such as chickpeas, haricot beans, and kidney beans
- grains such as brown rice and unrefined basmati rice

To drink, you can choose from one of the following:
- still or sparkling water
- one 3.5-fl-oz (10-cl) glass of wine or champagne
- one 3.5-fl-oz (10-cl) glass of beer

ON FRUIT

On the Rapid Weight Loss plan, you can enjoy a range of desserts made from fruit, since most fruits have low GI values of 35 and below. Fresh fruit or fruit compote made from apples, pears, apricots, and peaches, for example, can be a delicious sweet treat after a meal. You can also enjoy fresh raspberries, cherries, and strawberries directly after your meal, since they also have low GI values. Another fruit-based option is to stir a bit of sugar-free jam into some low-fat or fat-free yogurt. These low-fat desserts are ideal options following high-fiber carbohydrate meals.

On dessert

The main problem with classic desserts is that they are usually made with white flour, sugar, butter, or perhaps all three. But this does not mean that you have to forgo dessert completely when following the Diet—you simply have to choose your desserts wisely.

CHOCOLATE AND OTHER SWEET TREATS

During the Rapid Weight Loss plan, you may indulge in a wide variety of desserts. You must ensure, however, that the carbohydrates you use have a GI no higher than 35. Luckily, there are lots of healthy options open to you. For example, very few people know that dark chocolate (containing at least 70 percent cocoa) has a low GI of only 25. This means that you can enjoy a few squares of high-quality dark chocolate, or prepare desserts made from it, such as the decadent chocolate cake recipe listed at the back of this book (*see pp232–33*). It has a GI of 25, so you can enjoy it with a guilt-free conscience. So long as your sweet treat does not contain any food with a GI higher than 35, desserts are totally acceptable while following the Rapid Weight Loss plan.

You can also eat desserts made with eggs, low-GI fruits (*see left*), and fructose, since these are all low-GI foods. If you creatively base your recipes around these simple ingredients, you can make a wide range of tasty desserts, such as raspberry and chocolate mousse (*see p237*) and chocolate vanilla pots (*see p236*).

If you take a lateral approach to creating Rapid Weight Loss desserts, there's an endless range of possibilities open to you. For example, you can devise your own flan recipe using my recipe for cherry flan (from the *Montignac Provençal Cookbook*) as a template. Soak 1¾ lb (750 g) of pitted cherries in six tablespoons of rum. In a separate bowl, heat ¾ cup each of whipping cream and milk. Allow the milk and cream mixture to cool. In another bowl, beat together six eggs, ⅔ cup of fructose, and a drop of vanilla extract, and then add the milk and cream mixture to it, stirring constantly. Add the cherries and rum to this mixture and pour it into a 11-in (28-cm) quiche pan. Bake the flan at 275°F (130°C) for 50 minutes and chill in the refrigerator before serving.

CHEESE FOR DESSERT

In France, cheese is accorded the honor of being eaten with a knife and fork—a practice that should be encouraged throughout the world. This is because almost all cheeses have a negligible GI value. In other words, cheese contains very little, if any, sugar, and it will not contribute to weight gain. After a protein-fat lunch or dinner, just about every cheese is allowed—provided you eat it on its own, without any carbohydrates.

In many restaurants, the menu offers a dessert or cheese option. When dining out on the Rapid Weight Loss plan, you should limit yourself to the cheese option, since it's unlikely that any of the other desserts will be free from sugar and flour. Remember, though, you should always, always eat your cheese without bread or crackers. If you have high cholesterol, however, or if you have just eaten a high-fiber carbohydrate meal, you should only eat fat-free cheeses.

"In France, cheese is accorded the honor of being eaten with a knife and fork—a practice that should be encouraged throughout the world."

Left: the French consider cheese, such as Brie and Camembert, a delicious treat for dessert.

Dinner the Montignac way

Dinner on the Diet is almost identical to lunch in that it gives you two meal options: a protein-fat meal or a high-fiber carbohydrate meal. These are the same meal guidelines you were given for lunch—the only difference is that your dinner should be lighter than your lunch. In other words, both options should have more low-GI vegetables and less fat or high-fiber carbohydrates than your lunch portion. One caveat: if you have had a high-fiber carbohydrate meal for lunch, then it is best to balance it out by having a protein-fat meal for dinner.

Option 1
protein-fat dinner

This dinner option is almost exactly the same as the protein-fat lunch (*see pp86–87*), but its proportions should shift slightly. That is, the protein-fat dinner should be prepared with less fat, and it should include more low-GI vegetables, than the protein-fat lunch. You should eat this type of dinner on most evenings, since it has a good balance of very low-GI carbohydrates, proteins, and fats. The golden rule, though, is to avoid carbohydrates with GI values higher than 35.

SOUPS, APPETIZERS, AND SALADS

These dishes should contain lots of very low-GI vegetables, and they should be lighter on fat than your lunch appetizers and salads. Your appetizer can be a soup consisting of very low-GI vegetables or a selection of grilled, sautéed, or roasted vegetables with a sub-35 GI value. You can also have a side salad containing vegetables with very low GI values. Remember, it's perfectly acceptable for these dishes to contain fat (albeit less than you used at lunchtime), as long as they do not include carbohydrates with a GI higher than 35.

MAIN COURSE

As with the protein-fat lunch, the main course for your protein-fat dinner should be composed of a protein food, such as meat, fish, eggs, or chicken (prepared without carbohydrates such as bread crumbs or flour). Your dinner portion should be smaller than your lunch, though. It is also best to avoid having fatty meats for dinner, if possible, particularly if you have already had fatty meat, such as steak, for lunch; choose fish or lean meats, such as skinless chicken or lean pork instead. Drink a small glass of wine or beer with your meal and have some cheese or dark chocolate for dessert (*for more Rapid Weight Loss dessert options, see pp90–91*).

WHAT CAN I EAT?

The dinner to the left is a well-balanced protein-fat meal, consisting of a tomato and arugula salad, grilled asparagus and green onions (which are low-GI carbohydrates), and grilled tuna with Mediterranean marinade (see pp200–01), which fulfills the protein and fat requirements. Feel free to choose from the selection of foods below to create your ideal protein-fat dinner. Remember, you can prepare these foods with fat, if you wish.

For your sub-35 GI carbohydrate element, choose from the following:
- low-GI vegetables, such as broccoli, peppers, and spinach
- low-GI legumes and grains, such as lentils, quinoa, or wild rice

For your protein element, choose from the following:
- meat
- fish
- poultry
- eggs
- soy products such as tofu

To drink, you can choose one of the following:
- still or sparkling water
- one 3.5-fl-oz (10-cl) glass of wine or champagne
- one 3.5-fl-oz (10-cl) glass of beer

Option 2
high-fiber carbohydrate dinner

This meal is very low in fat, and it should be eaten no more than 3 to 4 times per week. It allows you to eat carbohydrates with a GI as high as 50, as long as you eat them with little or no fat. To ensure a well-balanced diet, have this type of dinner only on days when you have had a protein-fat lunch.

SOUPS, APPETIZERS, AND SALADS

You can start this meal with a non-creamy broth or puréed soup made with vegetables with a sub-35 GI value. Alternatively, you can prepare a selection of raw or steamed vegetables with a sub-35 GI value, such as broccoli, peppers, and celery. Do not add any saturated fats, such as butter, when preparing these dishes. You can also have a salad prepared with a dressing made from fat-free yogurt, mustard, and lemon juice. Alternatively, you may drizzle a very small amount of olive oil mixed with lemon juice or balsamic vinegar on your salad. Use as little oil as possible—or better yet, skip it altogether.

MAIN COURSE

The main element of your meal should be a high-fiber carbohydrate with a GI of 50 or below. Your main dish can include lentils, brown rice, wild rice, chickpeas, or whole-wheat spaghetti cooked *al dente*. A high-fiber carbohydrate main dish might be a mixed bean salad with peppers, tomatoes, and basil, drizzled with a little bit of olive oil (*see opposite*).

You should use very little, if any, fat when preparing this meal. If you do use a little oil, it should always be an unsaturated variety, such as olive oil. You may have a 3.5-fl-oz (10-cl) glass of wine, or a 3.5-fl-oz (10-cl) glass of beer to drink with your meal. For dessert, avoid high-fat options, such as cheese, and instead choose something low in fat, such as fat-free yogurt mixed with sugar-free jam.

WHAT CAN I EAT?

The dinner to the left is a well-balanced high-fiber carbohydrate meal. It includes a mixed bean salad with peppers, tomatoes, and basil, served with a side dish of grilled zucchini. Feel free to choose from the selection of foods below to create your ideal meal. This meal should be prepared with very little fat; avoid saturated fat altogether.

For your sub-35 GI carbohydrate element, choose from the following:
- low-GI vegetables, such as broccoli, peppers, and spinach
- low-GI legumes and grains, such as lentils, quinoa, and wild rice

For your high-fiber carbohydrate element, choose from the following:
- whole-wheat spaghetti (preferably served cold to reduce GI value)
- legumes such as chickpeas, haricot beans, and kidney beans
- grains such as brown rice and unrefined basmati rice

To drink, you can choose one of the following:
- still or sparkling water
- one 3.5-fl-oz (10-cl) glass of wine or champagne
- one 3.5-fl-oz (10-cl) glass of beer

GRAB AND GO SNACKS

If you have not had time to prepare anything at home, you can always pop into a delicatessen and buy the foods you need over the counter. Italian delicatessens are particularly good for this option, since they stock a wide array of meats and cheeses, all of which contain little or no sugar. These snacks are high in saturated fat, so they cannot be eaten with bread — not even wholemeal bread.

For instance, you could buy:

• cooked or dried ham
I particularly recommend Parma ham (*see right*), because it is cut very thinly, and any excess fat can be easily removed.

• turkey or chicken
It's best to choose skinless cuts of poultry whenever possible.

• dried sausage
Choose the leanest cut available and have it sliced for you in the shop, unless you happen to have a Swiss Army knife with you.

• hard-boiled eggs
If freshly prepared eggs aren't available, try them pickled.

• cheeses
All are suitable.

On snacks

If your midday meal has been sufficiently substantial, you should not feel the need to eat again before dinner. However, if you experience sharp hunger pangs, it is best to eat something. Whatever you do, never resort to eating high-GI carbohydrates, such as cookies, chips, bread, or popcorn. For weight loss, you must avoid carbohydrates with a GI above 35. The choices below are good snack options that will not undermine your weight loss plan.

PROTEIN IS ESSENTIAL

While it's important to choose very low-GI carbohydrates at snack time, the real key to keeping blood sugar levels, and your appetite, under control is to include at least a little protein as well. As I said earlier in the book (*see pp24–25*), protein, unlike carbohydrates, provides satiety, meaning it leaves you feeling fuller for longer than if you had eaten the same amount of carbohydrates. It is for this reason that I recommend choosing protein-based snack foods, such as meat or cheese, in addition to your sub-35, low GI carbohydrates.

Always be prepared!

Planning balanced snacks in advance can prevent you from making unhealthy snack choices. An ideal Rapid Weight Loss snack could include chopped raw vegetables, such as carrots, celery, tomatoes, and peppers, as well as slices of lean meats, and some cheese, such as cheddar or Gruyère. All of these foods can be eaten freely, since they have very low GI values.

Prepare this snack ahead of time, and carry it with you in a sealed plastic container. This way, you can head off dietary disaster and avoid grabbing some cookies and a cola in hunger-fueled, hypoglycemic (*see pp15–16*) desperation. If you're caught unprepared, you can always stop at a deli (*see panel, left*) and buy something there.

MEAT-FREE SNACKS

For a fast and easy option, you could have a snack consisting entirely of fresh or dried fruits with a GI of 35 or below. Eat as much as you like. The problem, however, with fruit is that it is quickly digested and you may soon feel hungry again. That is why for a grab-and-go snack, I recommend eating something rather more substantial, which contains protein, since the body digests protein more slowly than carbohydrates. Try nuts such as almonds (*see below*), hazelnuts, or walnuts. A low-fat liquid yogurt is another good snack option that contains protein.

rapid weight loss

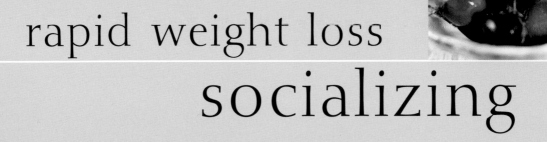

socializing

don't put a damper on party proceedings (or well-meaning friends who may cajole you into drinking with them). Don't tell anyone that you're abstaining from cocktails.

raise your glass to your lips as often as you would normally drink, but instead of drinking the alcohol, simply moisten your lips.

buy the first round of drinks, when out with your friends. Buy yourself a sparkling water with lime or a glass of tomato juice. As far as your friends know, you could be drinking a vodka and tonic or a bloody Mary!

_____ **choose red or white wine** or champagne over spirits for your apéritif, if you must drink. Wine and champagne contain less alcohol than spirits, and therefore they present less risk of jeopardizing your weight loss regimen.

_____ **accept a glass of good champagne** before your meal, should you be unable to do otherwise. Eat a few tidbits first, though, provided they do not contain any bad carbohydrates.

_____ **break open your roll** and then leave it uneaten on the side of your plate when at dinner parties. No one will notice!

_____ **indulge in cheese,** olives, deli meats, or smoked fish when faced with the canapé tray. Eat something, and then enjoy your glass of champagne or wine, guilt-free.

Rapid Weight Loss menu plan

If you need some inspiration for planning your Rapid Weight Loss meals and snacks, you can refer to the following sample seven-day menu plan for ideas.

This menu maps out a balanced variety of meals for each day. It includes three high-fiber carbohydrate meals, but you can have four, if you wish.

MEAL	DAY 1	DAY 2	DAY 3
Breakfast with herbal *or* fruit tea *or* decaffeinated coffee	• sugar-free jumbo oats with skim milk and strawberries	• whole-wheat toast with sugar-free jam • low-fat natural yogurt with raspberries	• oat cakes topped with fat-free cheese and sliced apples
Lunch with one 3.5-fl-oz (10-cl) glass dry wine *or* one 3.5-fl-oz (10-cl) glass beer	• Greek salad (salad greens, feta cheese, tomatoes, onions, and olive oil) • omelet made with Emmental cheese • a few squares of dark chocolate	• vegetable soup, e.g., broccoli soup • grilled zucchini • tricolor rice (*see p193*); mashed cauliflower • apples with cinnamon	• cherry tomato and basil soup (*see pp160–61*) • chef's salad (salad greens, cheese, ham, boiled egg, tomatoes, and olive oil) • a few squares of dark chocolate
Snack (optional)	• sugar-free yogurt drink	• egg salad and crudités	• almonds and hazelnuts
Dinner with one 3.5-fl-oz (10-cl) glass dry wine *or* one 3.5-fl-oz (10-cl) glass beer	• vegetable soup, e.g., puréed cucumber soup • green salad • broiled cod; sautéed broccoli • peach mousse (*see pp234–35*)	• soupe au vin blanc (*see p162*) • pork with herbed mustard (*see pp228–29*); steamed artichokes • sliced peaches with yogurt	• vegetable soup, e.g. puréed zucchini soup • wild mushroom ramekins (*see pp184–85*); arugula salad • chopped apples with yogurt

DAY 4

- toasted rye bread with sugar-free jam and fat-free cheese

- vegetable soup, e.g., mushroom soup
- French bean, artichoke, and arugula salad (see pp168–69)
- grilled chicken
- strawberries with yogurt

- crudités and Brie

- green salad
- grilled tuna; sautéed mushrooms
- natural yogurt with fresh sliced apricots

DAY 5

- sugar-free jumbo oats with skim milk and chopped apricots

- vegetable soup, e.g., broccoli soup
- green salad
- grilled steak; French beans;
- a few squares of dark chocolate

- pears with natural yogurt

- vegetable soup, e.g., mushroom soup
- green salad
- roast chicken; grilled asparagus
- Brie and Camembert

DAY 6

- omelet made with Gruyère cheese
- fried lardons

- vegetable soup, e.g., gazpacho
- green salad
- lentils with sautéed onion and mushrooms
- fat-free yogurt with sugar-free strawberry jam

- slices of ham and turkey

- soupe au vin blanc (see p162)
- sautéed eggplant
- grilled salmon with spinach
- a few squares of dark chocolate

DAY 7

- poached eggs
- grilled sausage

- vegetable soup, e.g., puréed pepper soup
- salad niçoise (salad greens, tuna, olives, boiled egg, capers, tomatoes, and olive oil)
- yogurt with pears

- crudités with crème fraîche

- vegetable soup, e.g., tomato soup
- steamed artichokes
- spaghetti with tomatoes and asparagus
- fat-free yogurt with fresh strawberries

Selection of good carbohydrates

Since carbohydrates are the only foods that contain sugar, GI values apply only to these foods. Fats and proteins (*see pp22–31*) contain very little sugar and their impact on blood sugar levels is negligible. The following is a small selection of good carbohydrate choices for the Rapid Weight Loss plan.

Avocados	10	Peppers (green)	15
Almonds	15	Peppers (red)	15
Asparagus	15	Peppers (yellow)	15
Artichokes	15	Pumpkin seeds	15
Brazil nuts	15	Spinach	15
Broccoli	15	Sunflower seeds	15
Brussels sprouts	15	Walnuts	15
Cabbage (all kinds)	15	Zucchini	15
Cauliflower	15	Eggplant	20
Celeriac	15	Fructose	20
Celery	15	Lemons	20
Cucumber	15	Limes	20
Fennel	15	Chinese vermicelli (soybean variety)	22
Hazelnuts	15	Beans, flageolet	25
Herbs	15	Blackberries	25
Leeks	15	Cherries	25
Lettuce (all kinds)	15	Dark chocolate (70 percent cocoa)	25
Mushrooms	15	Lentils (green)	25
Olives (all kinds)	15	Raspberries	25
Onions (all kinds)	15	Soybeans (cooked)	25
Peanuts	15	Split peas (yellow, cooked for 20 minutes)	25
Pecans	15	Strawberries	25

Apples (fresh)	30	Oranges	35
Apricots (fresh)	30	Peas (dried, cooked)	35
Beans, French	30	Peas (fresh, cooked)	35
Carrots (raw)	30	Plums	35
Chickpeas (cooked)	30	Prunes	35
Fruit jam (sugar-free)	30	Quinoa	35
Garlic	30	Wild rice	35
Grapefuit	30	Figs (dried)	40
Lentils (brown)	30		
Lentils (red)	30	**For the carbohydrate-protein breakfast, only:**	
Lentils (yellow)	30	Black bread (German)	40
Milk (reduced-fat or skim)	30	Bread made from whole-wheat flour	40
Mung beans (soaked and cooked for 20 minutes)	30	Rye bread	45
Nectarines	30	Whole-wheat bread with bran	45
Peaches	30		
Pears	30	**For high-fiber carbohydrate meals, only:**	
Tomatoes	30	Rice (unrefined basmati)	50
Apples (dried)	35	Rice (brown)	50
Apricots (dried)	35	Sweet potatoes	50
Beans, fava (peeled and cooked)	35	Spaghetti, durum-wheat (cooked *al dente*)	40
Beans, haricot	35	Spaghetti, whole-wheat (cooked *al dente*)	40
Clementines	35		
Figs (fresh)	35		
Kidney beans	35		
Natural yogurt	35		

WEIGHT
CONTROL PLAN

In a nutshell

This next section introduces you to some of the new rules you will be following on the Weight Control plan. The first thing you are likely to notice is that there are not many rules at all. That is because the defining characteristic of this plan is its flexibility. In fact, it is more a guide to good, healthy living, inspired by the French way of life. The longer you stay on the Weight Control plan, the easier choosing the right foods and maintaining your weight will become.

THE OBJECTIVES

The main purpose of the Weight Control plan is weight maintenance. That said, the Weight Control plan can be used in two different ways: first, it can be used after the Rapid Weight Loss plan to maintain your new weight and healthy pancreas. Second, if weight loss is not your main objective, you can skip the Rapid Weight Loss plan altogether, and jump straight into the Weight Control plan to maintain your current weight and the health of your pancreas.

Weight maintenance

On the Weight Control plan, you may eat carbohydrates with a GI up to 50 without gaining weight. Following this rule, as well as the other guidelines for this plan, will allow you to maintain your weight. If you have just lost weight on the Rapid Weight Loss plan, you should approach the Weight Control plan not as a separate eating plan, but instead as a more moderate and flexible extension of the Rapid Weight Loss plan. It is important for you to stick to most of the rules from the Rapid Weight Loss plan (*see pp48–49*) and gradually incorporate the new elements from the Weight Control plan over a period of a few weeks. If you are simply interested in maintaining your current weight, and are starting the Diet with the Weight Control plan, by all means implement all of the rules at once.

"The longer you stay on the Weight Control plan, the easier choosing the right foods and maintaining your weight will become."

The healthy pancreas

Now that you have a healthy pancreas, it is essential that you maintain it properly. If you slip into poor eating habits of eating bad, high-GI carbohydrates, your pancreas will simply become unhealthy. This will result in your entering a state of hyperinsulinism, and its accompanying sluggishness and weight gain.

Remember, being overweight is not caused by eating too much, but by eating the wrong foods. This, in turn, causes the body to produce too much insulin and store excess glucose as fat. If you follow the Weight Control guidelines, however, your pancreas should remain in good condition. In fact, the longer you follow the Diet, the better your pancreas will function, the easier it will be to maintain your weight, and the more relaxed you can be with your food choices.

Eat sub-50 GI for weight maintenance

The Weight Control plan encourages you to eat a wide variety of high-quality, delicious foods, and there are fewer rules and restrictions than on the Rapid Weight Loss plan. If you want to maintain your weight and the health of your pancreas, you must always choose foods with a GI of 50 or below. If you do, on rare occasions, eat a carbohydrate with a GI higher than this, minimize the damage by implementing the AGI principle (*see pp112–14*) and eating a very low-GI carbohydrate first. The diagram below shows how your weight is affected by the GI of the foods you eat.

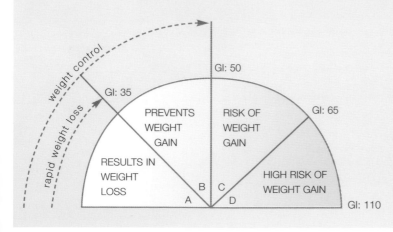

Zone A: GI of 35 and below results in weight loss

Zone B: GI of 36–50 prevents weight gain

Zone C: GI of 51–65 risk of weight gain

Zone D: GI above 65 high risk of weight gain

weight control
the rules

1 **maintain your weight** with this plan. It is actually a flexible extension of the Rapid Weight Loss plan. If you do not wish to lose weight, however, you can skip the Rapid Weight Loss plan, and jump straight into the Weight Control plan to maintain your weight and the health of your pancreas.

2 **keep both breakfast options:** the protein-carbohydrate breakfast and the protein-fat breakfast. The protein-carbohydrate breakfast is the healthier option and you should have it on most mornings.

3 **you may eat flexible main meals.** In other words, there are no more "meal options" for lunch or dinner. There is really one golden rule to bear in mind: always choose carbohydrates with a GI of 50 or below. If you want to include a carbohydrate with a GI higher than this, you must count it as a discrepancy (*see opposite and pp116–17*) or use the AGI principle (*see opposite and pp112–14*).

4
eat whole-wheat bread as part of the carbohydrate-protein breakfast and as a snack. However, because all bread, even good, whole-wheat bread, is very high in starch, these are the only times bread can be eaten on the Weight Control plan.

5
use the AGI principle, or the average glycemic index (*see pp112–14*), if you want to eat a carbohydrate with a GI higher than 50. It will reduce the effects of the high GI food on your blood sugar levels.

6
you can have two high-GI treats, or discrepancies (*see pp116–17*), per month without running the risk of gaining weight. This involves planning a chosen treat in advance, and minimizing the effects through a specially tailored plan of action.

7
have two small glasses of wine or one 12-fl-oz (33-cl) bottle of beer with your main meals each day, if you wish. You may have the occasional apéritif or after-dinner drink, in moderation (*see pp128–29*). Whatever you do, however, you must never drink alcohol on an empty stomach.

What is the AGI?

Eating good food is one of the supreme experiences of our existence, and cooking is a true art, in the same league as music or painting. This is why it would be a shame to deprive oneself forever of foods that, despite the fact that they may have a relatively high GI value, nonetheless have an important gastronomic dimension. By implementing the AGI (average glycemic index) principle, you will be able to eat some of these delicacies without gaining weight.

WHAT IS THE AGI PRINCIPLE?

The AGI is one of the most important aspects of the Weight Control plan. It is exactly what its name suggests: the average GI of all the carbohydrates eaten during the course of a meal. So it is not the GI value of any one particular carbohydrate you eat during a meal that matters most, but the combined effect that several carbohydrate foods have on one another. If you happen to eat a high-GI carbohydrate during the course of a meal, the outcome will not necessarily be a catastrophe for your blood sugar levels and your weight.

How does the AGI principle work?

The AGI is, in essence, your body's system of checks and balances, and it will allow you to eat certain high-GI foods, as long as they are accompanied (or preferably preceded by) some very low-GI, high-fiber carbohydrates. This means that if you eat a carbohydrate with a GI that is slightly higher than recommended (above 50 on the Weight Control plan), its effect on your pancreas will be reduced by eating another carbohydrate that has a very low GI value.

So, for example, a dish of potatoes will cause the glucose level in your blood to rise appreciably, whereas low-GI vegetables rich in fiber will cause glucose levels to rise only slightly. Eat the two together and the

THE AGI IN ACTION

This meal (see left) is a good illustration of the AGI principle. The formula below is not an exact science. It should only be used to get an approximation of the AGI, and not an exact figure. The dinner includes boiled potatoes (a very high-GI food), steamed broccoli (a very low-GI food), and grilled salmon. The broccoli will bring down the AGI of the potatoes, as long as you eat your carbohydrates in this order:

• **the broccoli** should be eaten first, since it has a low GI of 15. Its low GI will bring down the high GI of the potatoes.

• **the potatoes** should be eaten next. They have been boiled in their skins and have a high GI of 65. Add this GI value to that of the broccoli, and you get 80. To get an average glycemic index, or AGI, divide by two.

• **the AGI** of the two foods, when eaten together, is about 40, which is a perfectly acceptable AGI on the Weight Control plan.

• **it is worth noting** that the AGI should only be obtained through eating normal quantities of low-GI foods to compensate for high-GI foods, not huge amounts.

glucose level in your blood will increase to a level somewhere between the two extremes, depending on how much potato or low-GI, high-fiber vegetables you have eaten.

The limits of the AGI

This is not a cut-and-dried formula, and it should be viewed as a guideline only for how to eat carbohydrates with a GI higher than 50 on the Weight Control plan. To offset the potential damage of a high-GI food, you must always aim to implement the AGI principle by eating a very low-GI carbohydrate *before* you eat your high-GI carbohydrate. The order in which you eat your carbohydrates is key. If you eat your high-GI carbohydrate first, your blood sugar levels will remain high.

The AGI principle is a general guideline, and moderation is the key to using it to maintaining your weight. Too many carbohydrates, regardless of their GI values, will be transformed into body fat. If you eat a huge portion of potatoes, you should not eat an enormous portion of broccoli to "undo" the damage. You must consider not just the AGI, but also the concentration of carbohydrates (*see below*) contained in your meal.

The concentration of carbohydrates

The GI of a carbohydrate is important, but it needs to be seen in relation to the concentration of carbohydrates—that is, the number of grams of carbohydrates that a food contains. On checking the chart (*see opposite*) there are nice surprises in store. For instance, a cooked carrot has a high GI value of 85, but it has a low carbohydrate content of six grams per 3.5-oz (100-gram) serving. French fries, however, have a high concentration of carbohydrate of 33 grams per serving.

So a small portion of cooked carrots will have a minimal effect on your blood sugar levels. You would have to eat nearly 21 oz (600 grams) of cooked carrots to achieve the same blood sugar spike as 3.5 oz (100 grams) of fries. Other high-GI, low-carbohydrate foods include melon (6 g), turnips (3 g), and watermelon (7 g). On this plan, you do not have to be as vigilant about these foods. Provided you do not eat them too often and in too great a quantity, they will not cause you to gain weight.

"Eating good food is one of the supreme experiences of our existence, and cooking is a true art, in the same league as music or painting."

Concentration of carbohydrates

The concentration of carbohydrates is the number of grams of carbohydrates contained in a 3.5-oz (100-gram) serving of food. Foods with a high GI, but a low carbohydrate concentration (10 g or less per serving), are fine to eat in moderation on the Weight Control plan, and are marked by an asterisk below.

Food	Carbohydrate concentration	GI	Food	Carbohydrate concentration	GI
Apricots (dried)	63 g	35	Lentils (brown, red, yellow)	17 g	30
Apricots (fresh)	10 g	30	Lentils (green)	17g	25
Bananas (ripe)	20 g	60	Melon*	6g	60
Beans, green (string)	3 g	30	Milk (reduced-fat)	5g	30
Beans, haricot	17 g	35	Natural yogurt	5g	35
Beets*	10 g	65	Peanuts	9g	15
Carrots (cooked)*	6 g	85	Peas, dried	7g	35
Carrots (raw)	6 g	30	Potato (fried or French fries)	33g	95
Chickpeas (garbanzos)	22 g	30	Pumpkin*	7g	75
Chinese vermicelli (soybean variety)	15 g	22	Quinoa	35g	18
Cornflakes	85 g	85	Raisins	66g	65
Dark chocolate (70 percent cocoa)	32 g	25	Rice (unrefined basmati)	23g	50
Flour (white bread flour)	53 g	70	Rice (brown)	23g	50
Fructose	100 g	20	Rice cakes	24g	85
Golden raisins	66g	65	Rice (parboiled)	24g	70
Grapes (all kinds)	16 g	45	Soybeans (cooked)	15g	25
Honey	80 g	85	Sweet potato	20g	50
Jam (made with sugar)	70 g	65	Sugar (saccharose)	100g	70
Jam (sugar-free)	37 g	30	Spaghetti, durum wheat (al dente)	25g	40
Kidney beans	11 g	35	Turnips*	3g	70
Kiwi fruit	12 g	50	Watermelon*	7g	75

What are discrepancies?

This aspect of the Diet is closely tied to the AGI principle (*see pp112–14*). It is also one of the Diet's most subtle and complicated concepts to put into practice. Make sure you have a good understanding of the AGI before incorporating any discrepancies into your diet.

Q What exactly is a discrepancy?

A discrepancy is a planned deviation from the Diet. It allows you to occasionally eat foods with a GI much higher than 50. A discrepancy is not a binge or a failure of will because it is planned and deliberate. It is unique to this plan because your pancreas should be well enough to cope with the occasional high-GI food.

Q Is there anything I can't have?

No. Any relatively high-GI food may be considered a discrepancy, providing it fulfills two conditions: first, the food must be a genuine exception to the way you normally eat. Second, you should take into account the food's GI and its concentration of carbohydrates, and whenever possible, choose the "least bad" option.

Q How often can I include discrepancies?

I am loath to discuss discrepancies because people can misuse the concept and gain weight. Remember, this is your chance to enjoy your favorite foods, without guilt, on very special occasions. Therefore, it is essential that you do not abuse your discrepancy privilege, and that you limit them to no more than twice a month.

Q Is there a golden rule on discrepancies?

Yes. If you are planning to have a discrepancy, always finish your meal with one and never start with one. If you begin your meal with low-GI foods, followed by a high-GI food, the average GI will remain relatively low, stimulating a minimal insulin response. A high-GI food eaten at the beginning of the meal will cause blood sugar levels to remain high, even if you then eat a low-GI food. So have dessert after dinner, but never have bread before your meal.

Q How do I incorporate my discrepancies?

The trick is to deliberately plan to have your treat, and exercise extreme caution in your other food choices. For example, if you know you want a piece of traditional dessert (e.g., pie) after dinner, that is your planned discrepancy. Simply make certain that the rest of your meal contains very low-GI carbohydrates (and lean protein, for added satiety). Eat your low-GI, healthy carbohydrates first. Then you should enjoy your dessert, guilt-free, and savor every mouthful. The presence of high-fiber, low-GI carbohydrates will offset the damage done by lowering the AGI of your meal.

Q Are there any caveats?

Ideally, your discrepancies should consist of foods with a low concentration of carbohydrates, such as watermelon, since their impact on blood sugar levels is easier to balance out. But once you start distinguishing between big and small discrepancies, you run the risk of focusing your undivided attention on the big ones, while overlooking the small ones. Never lose sight of the fact that small discrepancies are still deviations, and they should not become a regular feature of your diet or you will gain weight.

Choose foods wisely

The Weight Control plan is a more relaxed extension of the Rapid Weight Loss plan (*see pp44–105*), but there are still some foods that should be treated with caution. This section will show you how to choose the right foods to maintain your weight.

- starches

- bread

- pasta

- fruit

- drinks

On starches

Even on the Weight Control plan, I remain staunchly opposed to certain starches, such as white potatoes, sticky white rice, and corn. These foods have high GI values, and eating them regularly will invariably lead to weight gain. However, not all starches are bad for you, and on this plan you can enjoy all of the good starches without rules or restrictions.

POTATOES

Sweet potatoes are rich in fiber, which gives them a medium GI of 50. This GI value makes sweet potatoes an acceptable food to eat freely on the Weight Control plan. Always eat them with the skin on to retain their fiber content and to ensure that their GI does not rise above 50.

A white potato, on the other hand, can have a GI value as high as 95, since it contains very little in the way of fiber. Given their high GI, it almost goes without saying that white potatoes are terrible for your weight, and should be avoided at all costs. If you must have potatoes, though, do so rarely, and always employ the AGI principle by eating some very low–GI, high-fiber vegetables first.

RICE AND OTHER GRAINS

Unrefined basmati rice, brown rice, and wild rice are rich in fiber, and they all have GI values of 50 and below. This means that you may eat any of these foods whenever you wish on the Weight Control plan. Wild rice, which is actually an oat and not a rice, is especially good since it has a very low GI of 35. Quinoa is another recommended low–GI grain option, since it also has a GI of 35.

Refined regular sticky white rice, however, is almost completely devoid of fiber. Its high starch, low-fiber content gives it a very high GI of at least 70, which is roughly the same GI as sugar itself. So this kind of white rice is banned, even on the Weight Control plan. If you do eat white rice, do so on rare occasions, and always consider it a discrepancy.

PASTA

The Weight Control plan permits you to eat pasta whenever you like, and not just as a part of certain specified meals. You can also eat white pasta, so long as it is made from durum wheat. If you are unsure if a pasta is made from drum or soft-grain wheat, then stick with whole-wheat pasta, which is a safe, relatively low-GI option. The best pastas, however, are pastified varieties (*see pp64–65*), such as spaghetti and linguini. Always cook your pasta so that it is *al dente*. The best pasta to choose, though, is Chinese vermicelli, made from soy flour. It has a very low GI of 22, which is the lowest GI of all pastas.

LEGUMES

All types of lentils and other legumes, such as chickpeas, haricot beans, French beans, and split peas, can be eaten freely throughout both plans of the Diet since they have very low GI values. Green, red, yellow, and brown lentils are particularly good choices, since their GI values are very low, ranging from 25 to 30. Kidney beans have a slightly higher GI value of 35, but they, too, can be eaten freely without fear of weight gain. All of these legumes are relatively low-GI foods that are high in fiber and can be eaten whenever you wish.

Can I eat bread?

Bread is a sticking point, even on the Weight Control plan. Some types of breads are very high in starch (with a carbohydrate concentration of 53 g per 3.5-oz/100-g serving) and sugar, and if you abuse them, you run the risk of destabilizing your pancreas and gaining weight. If you have lost weight on the Rapid Weight Loss plan, this Q&A section will give you all the information you need to help you avoid regaining all the weight you have lost.

Q Is bread still fattening on this plan?

The answer is a qualified yes. Certain types of bread, such as white bread, French bread, rolls, and croissants, will always wreak havoc on your waistline. Although your pancreas should be functioning properly, even a healthy pancreas cannot handle the burden of sugar and starch present in these high-GI breads. If you indulge in these foods no more than twice a month, as planned discrepancies (*see pp116-17*), then you should not experience any problems. Exceeding this limit, however, will destabilize your pancreas so that it secretes too much insulin, which will lead to weight gain.

Q Can I still eat bread for breakfast?

Yes. For the carbohydrate-protein breakfast, you should continue to eat only unrefined whole-wheat or rye bread. After about three months on the Weight Control plan, you may spread your bread with a little light margarine, if you wish. When eating your protein-fat breakfast option, however, you should avoid eating any bread—even if it happens to be good whole-wheat bread!

Q What kind of bread can I eat?

The good breads are rye or whole-wheat varieties, preferably made from unrefined, organic flour. However, white bread will always be banned from the Diet, even on the Weight Control plan. No matter how healthy your pancreas may be, regularly including white bread in your diet will always lead to weight gain and metabolic imbalance. During breakfast, lunch, or dinner, at home, at the cafeteria, or in a good restaurant, you should always obey the golden rule: no white bread!

Q When else can I eat bread?

On the Weight Control plan, you can eat unrefined whole-wheat or rye bread not just for breakfast, but as a snack, too. But these are the only times that bread is permitted. The snack is something I call the sandwich à la Montignac (*see pp144–45*). The bread should be whole-wheat or rye and it should be toasted, since toasting bread may reduce its GI value. Fill the sandwich with very low-GI vegetables, lean meats, and fat-free cheeses. Remember, this is a snack, not a side dish, and it should be eaten only on an empty stomach.

Q Can I ever eat another croissant?

If you love croissants or white bread, then make these foods one of your two discrepancies a month and it is unlikely that you will gain weight. On occasion, I find it impossible to resist delicious (but very high-GI) croissants oozing with butter. In such instances, at the end of the meal, I automatically take into account how my dietary balance has been upset. In other words, I will usually make a mental note of what I had for breakfast, and eat prudently and sensibly for the rest of the day.

On fruit

Whether you are on the Weight Control plan or the Rapid Weight Loss plan, sugar is considered poison on the Diet. Although fruit is full of vitamins and fiber, it also contains some sugar. It is therefore essential to monitor the GI of every piece of fruit you eat. Fortunately, most fruits have low GI values, and are therefore not only acceptable on the Weight Control plan, but recommended.

FRESH AND DRIED FRUIT

The rules for eating fruit on the Rapid Weight Loss plan (*see pp66–67*) also apply here. That is, you can eat fresh fruit, but be wary of its GI value. On the Rapid Weight Loss plan, you were only allowed those fresh fruits with a GI value of 35 and below. On the Weight Control plan, you may eat fruits with a GI as high as 50, but no higher than that. Luckily, most fresh fruits, such as apples, apricots, cherries, figs, and pears, have GI values that fall far below this limit. You can also enjoy kiwi fruit and grapes, which have GI values of 50 and 45, respectively. The list of high-GI fresh fruits is fortunately short, and it includes fruits such as melon and watermelon. Although these fruits have high GI values, because their concentration of carbohydrates (*see pp114–15*) is low, you may eat these foods in moderation on the Weight Control plan.

Uncooked dried fruits have a medium GI but contain a lot of good fiber. This means that they are ideal if you do a lot of vigorous exercise, such as jogging. Most dried fruits, including some of those found in muesli, are allowed on the Weight Control plan. Dried apricots and prunes are the best options, since they both have a low GI value of 35; dried figs (GI of 40) are also acceptable. Dried fruits to avoid include raisins, dried bananas, and dried coconut. Dried banana, in particular, is the worst dried fruit option for your waistline, as it has a high GI of 65.

FRUIT JUICE

Because commercially prepared fruit juices are high in sugar and low in fiber, they should be avoided at all costs. Even varieties that are labeled "freshly squeezed" may not be free from added sugar. What's more, many of these juices have the pulp removed, and pulp is where all the fiber is. Although it is far healthier to eat a piece of fruit whole, you may drink homemade fruit juices, such as freshly squeezed orange juice (*see below*), in moderation. It has a medium GI of 45 and will not contribute to weight gain. However, even freshly squeezed, homemade juices will be lower in fiber than their whole-fruit counterparts.

CANNED AND PRESERVED FRUITS

You may occasionally have low-GI fruit canned in water, with no sugar added. It is not an ideal fruit choice, since canned fruit is likely to contain artificial preservatives of some sort, and it contains less fiber than fresh and dried varieties. Fruits canned in syrup should be completely excluded because of the large amount of sugar added to make the syrup. In addition, fruit jams, sweetened with added sugar or grape juice, should be avoided throughout the Diet. Replace these high-GI spreads with sugar-free fruit jams sweetened with fructose or artificial sweeteners.

"Most dried fruits, including some of those found in muesli, are allowed on the Weight Control plan."

Left: kiwi fruit, grapes, apricots, and pears are all acceptable fruits for weight maintenance.

On drinks

Even on the Weight Control plan, caffeine and sugar can still upset your metabolism. This means that the basic rules for these beverages remain much the same as those for the Rapid Weight Loss plan (*see pp70–71*). However, since your pancreas is not as sensitive as it once was, you can afford to be a little less rigorous in your application of the rules.

SOFT DRINKS

Avoid soft drinks, even on the Weight Control plan. Regular varieties contain too much sugar and caffeine, and diet soft drinks contain artificial sweeteners that can have an effect similar to sugar on your blood sugar levels (*see p52*). In place of synthetic soft drinks, your preferred beverage should be a tall glass of sparkling water with a twist of lemon or lime.

TEA AND COFFEE

Throughout the Diet, avoid regular coffee and stick to the decaffeinated variety instead. Pure arabica coffee is another option: it is thought to be lower in caffeine than robusta coffee, the most common type of canned coffee. If you are a tea-drinker, you may continue to drink weak black tea or herbal or fruit teas. That said, on the Weight Control plan, you should have a higher tolerance threshold at which insulin is secreted, so a little caffeine will not dramatically harm your metabolic equilibrium.

MILK

Avoid whole milk, since it is a complex food, consisting of proteins, saturated fats, and carbohydrates (lactose, or milk sugars). The watery part of milk (whey, which contains lactose) triggers the pancreas to produce insulin, which can trap the milk's saturated fat in the body for storage as fat tissue. Stick to skim milk instead, since it does not contain any saturated fat.

ESPRESSO

Few people know that real coffee—Italian espresso—is not very high in caffeine. This is because the high pressure of steam causes the ground coffee to release its magnificent flavor in concentrated form without releasing too much caffeine at the same time.

On the Weight Control plan, when you have reached the goals you set yourself at the start, and your pancreas is functioning normally, you will be able to enjoy espresso, in moderation.

Allow yourself the occasional pleasure of drinking a really good espresso at the end of your meal, along with a couple of squares of dark chocolate, if you wish.

Can I drink alcohol?

On the Weight Control Plan, you may drink alcohol in a moderate and controlled way. This is because your pancreas should have recovered its natural equilibrium, discharging the right amount of insulin to control the levels of glucose in the bloodstream. The golden rule on drinking alcohol while following the Diet is to eat a protein-fat snack, such as cheese, before drinking anything.

Q How much wine and champagne can I drink?

On the Weight Control plan, you may drink up to four 3.5-fl oz (10-cl) glasses of wine or champagne per day (but not all at once!) without destabilizing your metabolism. If the GI of your meal has not exceeded 50, then feel free to indulge in a couple of glasses. As on the Rapid Weight Loss plan (*see pp72–73*), never drink on an empty stomach and always choose red wine, dry white wine, or good-quality champagne.

Q What about beer?

You may drink 12 fl oz (33 cl) of beer with food per main meal (i.e., lunch and dinner) on the Weight Control plan without gaining weight. However, remember that beer is high in sugar, and it is easily converted into fat reserves. As on the Rapid Weight Loss plan, you must refrain from drinking beer between meals. If you really cannot resist, approach the situation as you would any other discrepancy. That is, drink a couple of glasses of the very best beer available—but never do it on an empty stomach!

Q Can I have apéritifs?

Yes, so long as you indulge in moderation and eat a protein-fat snack first. Choose a high-quality red wine or champagne rather than a high-proof alcohol, such as vodka. The effects will be less serious, since the amount of alcohol contained in a glass of spirits is roughly equivalent to three or four glasses of red wine or champagne. If you must have a spirit-based apéritif, drink it straight (or mixed with water) and limit yourself to one.

Q Are after-dinner drinks acceptable?

If your meal has been accompanied by one small 3.5-fl oz (10-cl) glass of wine, a small quantity of cognac or sherry at the end will not have a catastrophic effect. However, if you drink a glass of cognac that rivals the size of a swimming pool, I would prefer not to be held responsible for the results—particularly if you have also consumed four or five glasses of wine during the course of your meal. Remember, though, that a generous glass of spirits is equivalent to about three or four glasses of wine.

BENEFITS OF WINE

Many scientific studies have shown that wine, particularly red wine, has medicinal and protective properties. The beneficial effect of wine is due mainly to its powerful antioxidants, which offer valuable protection against byproducts of the metabolic process. When consumed in moderate amounts, the antioxidants in wine may prevent the development of some cancers, cardiovascular disease, and even Alzheimer's disease. In addition, wine may improve the way your pancreas responds to glucose in the bloodstream, which helps to reduce hyperinsulinism.

weight control
digested chapter

maintain your weight and the health of your pancreas with the Weight Control plan.

implement Weight Control rules gradually, over several months, to avoid overburdening your pancreas. The Weight Control plan should be viewed as a flexible extension of the Rapid Weight Loss plan.

eat carbohydrates with a GI up to 50 without fear of gaining weight or destabilizing your pancreas.

have any protein or fat you want with carbohydrates that have a GI of 50 or below. Flexibility is the hallmark of this plan, and there are no restrictive meal options for lunches and dinners.

use the AGI to eat the occasional carbohydrate with a GI slightly higher than 50, as long as you implement the AGI principle (*see pp112–14*), and eat it with high-fiber, low GI vegetables.

you can drink wine, up to four 3.5-fl-oz (10-cl) glasses, or two 12-fl-oz (33-cl) bottles of beer, per day (but never on an empty stomach). You can also enjoy the occasional espresso, if you wish.

enjoy whole–wheat bread for breakfast and in the form of a snack called the sandwich à la Montignac (*see pp144–45*). However, this is meant to be a snack, and bread (even good bread) should not be eaten at any other time of the day.

you may have two planned high-GI treats called discrepancies (*see pp116–17*) per month without fear of gaining weight. If possible, try to choose a treat with a low carbohydrate concentration (*see p115*), and eat some low-GI, healthy carbohydrates first; then eat virtuously for the rest of the meal and the day.

WEIGHT CONTROL:
MEAL OPTIONS

On breakfast

Breakfast on the Diet is a hearty meal that will not contribute to weight gain. On the Weight Control Plan (as on the Rapid Weight Loss plan), there are two possible breakfast options: the carbohydrate-protein meal, which is built around good carbohydrates and a low-fat or fat-free protein source, and the protein-fat breakfast, which is high in protein and saturated fats and free from carbohydrates. The carbohydrate-protein breakfast is still the healthier option of the two, and it should be eaten at least five days a week.

OPTION 1 carbohydrate-protein breakfast

The carbohydrate-protein breakfast from the Rapid Weight Loss plan (*see pp80–81*) should be your staple breakfast on the Weight Control Plan. It contains very little saturated fat, a low-fat or fat-free protein, and a

Right: *jumbo oats with skim milk and fresh berries is an ideal carbohydrate-protein breakfast.*

high-fiber, low-GI carbohydrate. It may also include some low-GI fruit, if you wish. By combining acceptable carbohydrate and protein elements (*see below*), you can create such a diverse range of healthy and delicious breakfasts that it is unlikely that you will ever tire of this meal option.

For your carbohydrate element, look for foods that are rich in fiber and low in sugar. Some good examples of acceptable carbohydrate options include whole-wheat bread, rye bread, bread made with unrefined organic flour, sugar-free oat cakes, or sugar-free whole-grain cereal, such as jumbo oats. If, after about three months on the Weight Control Plan, you have grown tired of spreading your toast with sugar-free jam or jelly, you may use a light margarine instead.

For your protein element, choose protein-rich foods that are very low in, or completely free from, saturated fat. Skim milk or fat-free varieties of natural yogurt, cheese, and cottage cheese are all good protein options. If you have a sweet tooth, you can add a little sugar-free jam to your morning yogurt.

OPTION 2 protein-fat breakfast

The protein-fat meal is an ideal choice for a relaxed and indulgent weekend breakfast. It consists of proteins and saturated fats, and should be completely free from carbohydrates. However, its high saturated fat content means this meal should be eaten no more than twice a week.

The protein portion of this meal can be ham, fish, cheese, or eggs. Eggs can be scrambled, boiled, fried, or made into an omelet. Scrambled eggs and sausage make a perfect protein-fat meal that will keep you feeling satisfied until lunch. (*For more options, see pp82–83.*) You can use fats such as butter in the preparation of this meal, and you can also have high-fat foods such as bacon with it. Eat as much as you like, so long as your breakfast does not include any carbohydrates with a GI higher than 35.

Because this breakfast is very high in fat, it is essential to balance this meal throughout the day by selecting foods for lunch and dinner that are rich in good carbohydrates and low in saturated fats.

"The protein-fat meal is an ideal choice for a relaxed and indulgent weekend breakfast."

CARBOHYDRATES AND THE GI

An enormous range of carbohydrate foods is open to you on the Weight Control plan. Eat whatever type of carbohydrate you like with any type of protein or fat, so long as the carbohydrate has a GI of 50 or below. Good carbohydrates include lentils, pasta (cooked *al dente*), brown rice, wild rice, and sweet potatoes. However, it is a good idea to include some high-fiber, very low-GI vegetables in your meal, since they tend to be richer in vitamins than foods such as spaghetti and brown rice. The high levels of fiber they contain will also bring down the AGI (*see pp112–14*) of your meal.

Right, opposite: try lean roast beef, grilled mushrooms, and broccoli for a hearty Weight Control lunch.

On lunch

Lunch on the Weight Control plan is a far more flexible affair than it was on the Rapid Weight Loss plan, since there are no longer protein-fat or high-fiber carbohydrate meal options. There is simply one golden rule, and that is to keep the GI of your entire meal at or below 50. Do this, and you will maintain your weight and your healthy pancreas.

Have a filling lunch

The Weight Control lunch may consist of a soup, salad, side dish, and an entrée. You may also have wine or beer and a Montignac-approved dessert, if you wish (*for dessert options, see pp140–41*). Eat as much as you like; this meal should be filling enough to keep you going until dinner. Your lunch should be made up of carbohydrates with a GI of 50 or below, some fat, and some protein in the form of meat, chicken, fish, tofu, or eggs. Eat any type of carbohydrate you like, as long as it has a GI of 50 or below. Do not skimp on very low-GI vegetables. They contain valuable nutrients that reduce the AGI (*see box, left*) of your meal.

Balance and moderation is key

The Weight Control lunch may include carbohydrates such as pasta (cooked *al dente*) or brown rice, if you wish. You can even prepare your food with oil or cream, within reason; do not drown your salad in oil or douse everything in cream. There are no restrictions on the type or amount of protein you choose, but it should always be prepared without bread crumbs or flour. For a balanced diet, aim to eat a wide variety of protein-rich foods, such as fish, poultry, meat, and eggs.

Saturated fats (found in fatty meats and cream) should still be eaten in moderation, since they can contribute to cardiovascular disease. Always trim any visible fat from your meat, and whenever possible, use unsaturated, good fats such as olive oil and sunflower oil in place of saturated varieties.

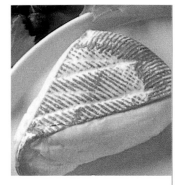

CHEESE

One of the great things about the Weight Control plan is that you may eat cheese for dessert following any lunch or dinner. (On the Rapid Weight Loss plan, you were advised not eat full-fat cheese following a high-fiber carbohydrate meal.) The reason for this new flexibility is that your pancreas should be functioning normally on this plan. In other words, after eating carbohydrates with a GI up to 50, your pancreas will not secrete an excess of insulin, and it will therefore not trap and store the saturated fat contained in the cheese.

On dessert

This section is very dear to me since I have a sweet tooth and am, by nature, a great lover of desserts at the end of a meal. As you might expect, all the desserts permitted on the Rapid Weight Loss plan are also allowed on the Weight Control plan. This plan is quite relaxed about desserts, provided you eat only foods with a GI of 50 or below. Luckily, this encompasses plenty of delicious options.

Nouvelle pâtisserie

Alongside the desserts you were allowed on the Rapid Weight Loss plan (*see pp90–91*)—fresh and cooked fruit, low-fat and fat-free natural yogurt, dark chocolate (70 percent cocoa), and cheese (*see box, left*)—you can also indulge in "nouvelle pâtisserie" (the nouvelle cuisine of desserts) on occasion. Just as nouvelle cuisine sauces seldom contain flour, nouvelle pâtisserie, especially the mousses, are made with very little sugar and hardly any flour.

French desserts

Perhaps I may be forgiven for claiming that French pastries are currently the best in the world for their originality, their beauty, their natural flavors and, above all, their lightness. Within the framework of this eating method, you are allowed to indulge in these delicacies throughout the Weight Control plan. If you love pastries, try to eat only the lightest ones, which are, by the way, also the best ones. Those containing the least sugar and flour are most compatible with the Diet's eating principles. Chocolate mousses made from dark bitter chocolate have few carbohydrates, and are particularly tasty.

For home chefs, the recipe for raspberry and chocolate mousse (*see p237*) is delicious. It contains very few carbohydrates, and has a very low GI value. It can be eaten freely, not only on the Weight Control plan, but even occasionally on the Rapid Weight Loss plan.

If you prefer cake, confine yourself to the very best chocolate cakes available. For example, a bitter chocolate fondant requires very little flour for a large cake. No sugar is added. The small amount of sugar in the chocolate is enough to make this cake an epicurean delicacy; one that will cause only a slight upset in your diet.

For those of you who like to create your own desserts from scratch, the chocolate cake recipe in the back of this book (*see pp232–33 and below*) is rich and decadent, but it contains no flour or added sugar at all. It derives its sweetness only from the dark chocolate it contains. It is therefore acceptable to eat for dessert on the Weight Control plan.

In fact, none of the desserts in the recipe section at the back of this book (*see pp232–37*) have high GI values, and all of them are acceptable for both plans on the Diet. To put it in perspective, almost any dessert you choose (from this book or your favorite restaurant) will cause less damage to your system than one horrible white potato.

> "If you love pastries, try to eat only the lightest ones, which are, by the way, also the best ones."

Left: *Montignac's chocolate cake (see pp232–33) is a delicious, low-GI dessert.*

On dinner

The Weight Control dinner is very similar to the Weight Control lunch. This plan does not include protein-fat and high-fiber carbohydrate meal options—there is only one firm rule, and that is to eat carbohydrates with a GI of 50 or below. The only real difference between lunch and dinner is that your dinner should be lighter than your lunch.

CARBOHYDRATES AND THE GI

As with lunch, you can eat whatever type of carbohydrate you want, so long as it has a GI of 50 or below. This might include unrefined basmati rice, brown rice, spaghetti cooked *al dente*, chickpeas, kidney beans, or lentils. Do not skimp on high-fiber, very low-GI vegetables, since they provide a wide range of nutrients, and the fiber they contain will bring down the AGI (*see pp112–14*) of your meal.

Have a light dinner

Since most people's activity levels are lowest in the evening, fats eaten at night are more easily stored as body fat. Dinner should, therefore, be your lightest meal of the day. It should contain less fat and more vegetables than lunch, and if you want to have protein in the evening, it is preferable to choose fish or lean meats instead of fatty cuts. Fresh cod and Parma ham rolls (*see opposite and pp204–205*), served with salad and red wine, is an excellent example of a Weight Control dinner.

Like lunch, the Weight Control dinner may consist of a soup, salad, side dish, entrée, dessert (*for Weight Control dessert options, see pp140–41*). To drink, you can have red wine, white wine, or beer, if you wish. Your dinner may include carbohydrates with a GI of 50 or below, as well as fats and protein in the form of lean meat, poultry, fish, tofu, or eggs. Take the time to enjoy each mouthful. Eat until you are full, but listen to your body and try not to overeat.

Fat and protein

Prepare your carbohydrates and proteins with any type of oil or fat you prefer, but try to use less of it than you did for your lunch. Remember, your body does not need fat in the evening, and it could be stored as body fat while you sleep. When choosing a protein, you should favor lean cuts of meat, removing any visible fat. Eggs, and especially fish, are also good options. Even fatty fish is fine because the kind of oil it contains will almost never be converted to fat.

Right, opposite: Fresh cod and Parma ham rolls (see pp204–205) makes a healthy Weight Control dinner.

On snacks

Your meals should be hearty enough to keep you going,
but if you feel the need for a snack, by all means have one.
However, you should never reach for cookies or chips to stave
off hunger pangs. For weight maintenance, the key to snacking
lies in choosing healthful foods with a GI no higher than 50.
The suggestions below are good snack options that will not
destabilize your pancreas or cause you to gain weight.

Quick snacks

All of the very low-GI snack foods allowed while following the Rapid
Weight Loss plan (*see pp98–99*) are also permitted on the Weight Control
plan. Snack on a handful of nuts, such as almonds, hazelnuts, or walnuts,
or on a low-fat, sugar-free yogurt drink. You could even have a snack
consisting only of fruit—eat as much as you like, as long as its GI value
is 50 or below.

Alternatively, you could always stop at a deli counter and order some
boiled eggs or sliced meats and cheeses and eat them on their own,
without bread or crackers. The proteins and fats these foods contain
should keep you full for a few hours without increasing your blood
sugar levels and eliciting an insulin response.

Prepared snacks

If you like to plan ahead, you could prepare a wide variety of chopped
raw vegetables such as carrots, tomatoes, and peppers, lean meats such as
turkey or ham, and enjoy them with some cheese, such as Cheddar,
Gruyère, or Brie.

You could even throw together a salad *niçoise* to snack on (made with
lettuce, boiled eggs, tuna, tomatoes, anchovies, and black olives, drizzled
with lemon juice and olive oil). If you prepare your snack ahead of time
and carry it with you in a sealed container, you can avoid hunger attacks,
and snack sensibly regardless of where you are.

SANDWICH À LA MONTIGNAC

Snacks on the Weight
Control plan can include bread in
the form of the sandwich à la
Montignac. Always use whole-wheat
or rye bread, and toast it to slightly
reduce its GI value. Between your
two slices of bread you can have
lean protein and any carbohydrate
you like, provided it has a GI of 35
or below. However, you must avoid
having any fats with it, except
perhaps a little olive oil. One caveat:
this sandwich is meant to be a light
snack, eaten on an empty stomach.
Filling suggestions include:

- **fish,** such as herring, tuna, and
  smoked salmon

- **lean meats,** including skinless
  chicken and turkey

- **low-GI vegetables,** such as
  lettuce, mushrooms, cucumber,
  raw carrots, peppers, and onions

- **sugar-free mustard** or
  horseradish

- **low-GI legumes,** including
  chickpeas and lentils

- **low-fat dairy products,**
  such as fat-free natural yogurt and
  low-fat cheese

weight control

socializing

_____ **be demanding** when dining at restaurants. Request that your meal be prepared without flour. It is always more effective to tell your waiter that you are allergic to flour than to say you are on a diet.

_____ **at dinner parties** wait as long as possible into the meal before drinking any alcohol. Choose red wine if you can, pair it with some cheese, and drink no more than absolutely necessary.

_____ **if served pâté on toast** at a dinner party, you can eat the pâté, which is generally a protein-fat, and leave the toast discreetly on the side of your plate. No one will notice!

_____ **at cocktail parties** it is easier than you might think to "lose" your drink somewhere in the room. Place your glass on a surface near someone with an empty glass, and see how long it is before your glass is absent-mindedly picked up by an appreciative party guest.

_____ **canapés** are out of the question, since the base is usually composed of a bad carbohydrate. However, it often supports a slice of salmon, sausage, or boiled egg. Simply disassemble the canapé and eat only the good carbohydrate, fat, or protein contained on top.

_____ **cunning tactics** are not always required at cocktail parties. Remember, any type of cheese is a good snack option, as is ham or sausage. So, too, are the ubiquitous cocktail sausages, spiked through with a toothpick and ready for consumption.

_____ **come prepared** if you feel that you will not be able to resist the culinary delights offered at a party. Take the edge off your appetite by having a protein-fat snack before you leave home.

COCKTAIL TIPS

When at a cocktail party, always have a small protein-fat snack, such as cheese (*see left*), before drinking any alcohol. When you drink on an empty stomach, the alcohol goes more rapidly into your bloodstream. This hinders weight loss and can even contribute to weight gain. In addition, if you must have an alcoholic apéritif, make it one of the following:

• **champagne** is the most acceptable alcoholic beverage to drink before a meal, but you must always have a protein-fat snack before taking your first sip. Never have more than one glass before you eat a meal, though.

• **dry red wine** is the next best type of alcohol you can choose. It is rich in antioxidants (*see pp130–31; 246*) and may help improve your tolerance to glucose. Again, limit yourself to only one glass before a meal, and always eat a protein-fat tidbit first.

• **dry white wine** is almost as good as dry red wine, but it lacks the powerful antioxidants found in red wine. Never have more than one glass with your protein-fat snack.

Weight Control menu plan

The Weight Control plan is not a diet in the strict sense of the word. It is not concerned with limiting quantities of food or calories. Instead, it is a set of flexible guidelines for making good food choices. Use the following menu plan if you need some inspiration when planning your Weight Control meals and snacks.

MEAL	DAY 1	DAY 2	DAY 3
Breakfast with herbal *or* fruit tea *or* decaffeinated coffee	• whole-wheat toast with sugar-free marmalade • low-fat natural yogurt with raspberries	• sugar-free jumbo oats with skim milk and berries	• oat cakes topped with fat-free cheese and sliced apples
Lunch with two 3.5-fl-oz (10-cl) glasses dry wine *or* one 12-fl-oz (33-cl) glass beer	• vegetable soup, e.g., cream of asparagus soup • green salad • linguini with ratatouille (*see p194*) • a few squares of dark chocolate	• vegetable soup, e.g., cream of cauliflower soup • broccoli sautéed with garlic and toasted walnuts • tricolor rice (*see p193*); grilled mushrooms • pears poached in red wine	• cherry tomato and basil soup (*see pp160–61*) • shrimp à la pastis (*see p202*); brown rice with feta cheese • a few squares of dark chocolate
Snack (optional)	• hazelnuts and almonds	• sandwich à la Montignac (*see pp144–45*)	• natural yogurt mixed with strawberries
Dinner with two 3.5-fl-oz (10-cl) glasses dry wine *or* one 12-fl-oz (33-cl) glass beer	• vegetable soup, e.g., mushroom soup • pork chops in caper sauce (*see pp224–25*); spinach sautéed with garlic • chocolate cake (*see pp232–33*)	• soupe au vin blanc (*see p162*) • cod on a bed of lentils (*see p198*); steamed artichokes • chopped apples mixed with yogurt	• lentil and lardon soup (*see p164*) • green salad • Montignac Gruyère quiche (*see pp186–87*) • raspberry and chocolate mousse (*see p237*)

DAY 4

- toasted rye bread
  with fat-free cheese

- soupe au vin blanc
  (see p162)
- leek and asparagus salad
  (see pp166–67)
- grilled salmon; baked
  sweet potato
- peaches poached in wine

- Camembert and
  sliced apples

- soupe au vin blanc
  (see p162)
- roast turkey; brown rice
  with grilled zucchini
- a few squares of dark
  chocolate

DAY 5

- sugar-free jumbo oats
  with skim milk
  and peaches

- eggplant, basil, and
  cannellini soup (see p163)
- lentils with sautéed
  mushrooms
- veal fillet in Gorgonzola
  sauce (see pp222–23)
- fresh figs and Brie

- selection of sliced meats

- vegetable soup, e.g.,
  mushroom soup
- goat cheese salad (see
  pp172–73)
- coq au vin (see pp210–11)
- natural yogurt with
  strawberries

DAY 6

- omelet made with goat
  cheese and spinach
- fried bacon

- green salad
- chicken with figs
  (see pp208–09)
- fat-free yogurt mixed with
  fresh raspberries

- sandwich à la Montignac
  (see pp144–45)

- vegetable soup, e.g.,
  tomato soup
- sautéed artichoke hearts
- penne with capers and
  olives (see p195)
- yogurt with fresh
  strawberries

DAY 7

- poached eggs
- grilled sausage

- cherry tomato and basil
  soup (see p160–61)
- green salad
- daube de boeuf
  (see p219)
- peaches with natural
  yogurt

- crudités with a low-fat
  hummus dip

- vegetable soup, e.g.,
  puréed cucumber soup
- grilled salmon; artichoke
  hearts with goat cheese
  (see pp180–81)
- Brie and apricots

Selection of good carbohydrates

Since carbohydrates are the only foods that contain sugar, GI values apply only to these foods. Fats and proteins (*see pp22–31*) contain very little, if any, sugar, so their impact on blood sugar levels is negligible. The following is a small selection of foods that can be eaten freely on the Weight Control plan.

Avocados	10	Pecans	15
Almonds	15	Peppers (green)	15
Asparagus	15	Peppers (red)	15
Artichokes	15	Peppers (yellow)	15
Brazil nuts	15	Pumpkin seeds	15
Broccoli	15	Spinach	15
Brussels sprouts	15	Sunflower seeds	15
Cabbage (all kinds)	15	Walnuts	15
Cauliflower	15	Eggplant	20
Celeriac	15	Fructose	20
Celery	15	Lemons	20
Courgettes	15	Limes	20
Cucumber	15	Chinese vermicelli (soybean variety)	22
Fennel	15	Beans, flageolet	25
Hazelnuts	15	Blackberries	25
Herbs	15	Cherries	25
Leeks	15	Dark chocolate (70 percent cocoa)	25
Lettuce (all kinds)	15	Lentils (green)	25
Mushrooms	15	Raspberries	25
Olives (all kinds)	15	Soya beans (cooked)	25
Onions (all kinds)	15	Split peas (yellow, cooked for 20 minutes)	25
Peanuts	15	Strawberries	25

Apples (fresh)	30	Oranges	35
Apricots (fresh)	30	Peas (dried, cooked)	35
Beans, French	30	Peas (fresh, cooked)	35
Carrots (raw)	30	Plums	35
Chickpeas (cooked)	30	Prunes	35
Fruit jam (sugar-free)	30	Quinoa	35
Garlic	30	Wild rice	35
Grapefuit	30	Black bread (German)	40
Lentils (brown)	30	Bread made from whole-wheat flour	40
Lentils (red)	30	Figs (dried)	40
Lentils (yellow)	30	Sherbet (sugar-free)	40
Milk (reduced-fat or skim)	30	Spaghetti, durum-wheat (cooked *al dente*)	40
Mung beans (soaked and cooked for 20 minutes)	30	Spaghetti, whole-wheat (cooked *al dente*)	40
Nectarines	30	Buckwheat	45
Peaches	30	Bulgur wheat (whole-grain, cooked)	45
Pears	30	Grapes (all kinds)	45
Tomatoes	30	Rye bread (whole-grain)	45
Apples (dried)	35	Orange juice (freshly squeezed)	45
Apricots (dried)	35	Whole-wheat bread with bran	45
Beans, fava (peeled and cooked)	35	Apple juice (fresh)	50
Beans, haricot	35	Crêpes (made with buckwheat)	50
Clementines	35	Kiwi fruit	50
Figs (fresh)	35	Rice (unrefined basmati)	50
Kidney beans	35	Rice (brown)	50
Natural yogurt	35	Sweet potatoes	50

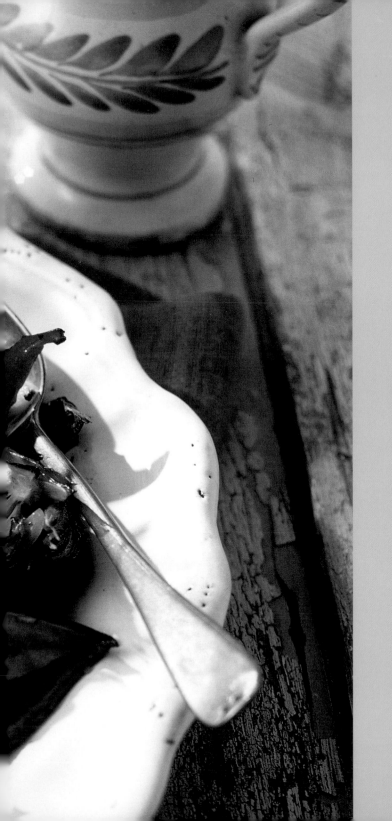

MONTIGNAC RECIPES

cooking
Montignac-style

use low-GI carbohydrates when you cook, since they prevent weight gain. Good examples include vegetables, such as broccoli, cabbage, spinach, and zucchini; legumes, including lentils and chickpeas; unrefined cereals and low-GI fruits.

eliminate high-GI carbohydrates when preparing meals. Foods to avoid include sugar, bread crumbs, white flour, white potatoes, corn, white rice, and white pasta such as ravioli, tortellini, and macaroni.

use good fats in your cooking whenever possible. These include olive oil, sunflower oil, walnut oil, pumpkinseed oil, goose fat, and duck fat (*for a more extensive list, see p41*).

eliminate bad fats from your cooking whenever possible. These include butter, coconut oil, palm oil, peanut oil, beef and pork drippings, lard, and hard stick margarine (*for a more extensive list, see p41*).

avoid bread crumbs and flour when cooking. Although any kind of cheese is acceptable, Parmesan makes a good substitute for bread crumbs. For sauces, replace white flour with puréed mushrooms or flour made from chickpeas, lentils, or soybeans.

add flavor to your cooking with red and dry white wine. They will not elicit a large insulin response or cause you to gain weight.

never use flour, butter, or sugar when making desserts. Instead, use sugar-free fruit purée, eggs, plain yogurt, dark chocolate, fructose, and "flour" made from ground almonds or hazelnuts.

Appetizers

Montignac appetizers, which include soups, salads, and vegetable dishes, should contain very low-GI vegetables and be free from high-GI carbohydrates, such as white potatoes and white rice. Most of the recipes in this section are acceptable for both the Rapid Weight Loss plan and the Weight Control plan (except where noted for Weight Control only).

SERVES 4

PREPARATION TIME
5 minutes

COOKING TIME
30 minutes

INGREDIENTS
1½ lb (600 g) cherry tomatoes
Good-quality olive oil
1 tsp chopped fresh thyme
3 garlic cloves, grated or cut
on a mandolin
3 celery sticks, chopped
2 leeks, chopped
2 white onions, chopped
1 tbsp tomato paste
good handful of fresh basil
14 oz (400 g) canned
tomatoes, roughly chopped
1¼ cups water or vegetable
stock

ACCEPTABLE FOR
RAPID WEIGHT LOSS
and
WEIGHT CONTROL

Cherry tomato and basil soup

The deep, rich red color of this flavorful soup is maintained by pushing it through a coarse sieve, rather than whizzing it in a blender or liquidizer. The latter method incorporates more air, meaning your soup will end up more orange than red.

1 Preheat the oven to 500°F (250°C) or its hottest possible setting. Arrange the cherry tomatoes on a baking sheet and drizzle with a little olive oil. Sprinkle with the thyme and garlic. Roast in the oven for 8 minutes.

2 Meanwhile, heat a large, heavy-based saucepan or soup pot over high heat. Drizzle in a little olive oil, then add the celery, leek, and onion. Sweat with the lid on for a few minutes, until softened but not colored. Add the tomato purée and basil stalks only.

3 Add the chopped tomatoes with their juice to the pan, then add the cherry tomatoes. Pour in the water, reduce the heat, and simmer slowly for 20 minutes.

4 Push the soup through a coarse strainer, discarding any skin and stalks. Return to the pan, adding salt to taste, and reheat gently.

5 Serve the soup hot in warmed bowls, with the shredded basil leaves sprinkled over the top and a drizzle of a little extra olive oil.

SERVES 4

PREPARATION TIME
5 minutes

COOKING TIME
20 minutes

INGREDIENTS

1 tbsp good-quality olive oil

6 shallots, finely chopped

1 lb (400 g) button
mushrooms, sliced

½ bottle dry white wine

3 tbsp tarragon vinegar

4 cups good-quality white
chicken stock (homemade is
best)

1 lb (500 g) ground almonds

2½ cups heavy cream

3 tbsp chopped fresh
tarragon

ACCEPTABLE FOR

RAPID WEIGHT LOSS

and

WEIGHT CONTROL

Soupe au vin blanc

It is important to keep the color of this soup as white as possible, so either make your own white chicken stock with no carrots or ensure that you buy a good-quality stock that is not too yellow and preferably also without carrots.

1   Drizzle the olive oil into the bottom of a large, heavy-based saucepan over high heat. Sprinkle in the shallot, cover the pan with a lid, and sweat for a couple of minutes, until the shallot is softened but not colored.

2   Add the mushroom, wine, and tarragon vinegar. Allow the wine to reduce a little while stirring, then add the chicken stock and bring the liquid to a boil.

3   Whisk in the ground almonds and bring the soup back to a boil. Allow the soup to thicken a bit—this will bring out the gluten in the almonds—then whisk in the cream and bring back to a boil once again.

4   Skim off any scum, reduce the heat, and add salt to taste. Sprinkle in the tarragon and stir through.

5   Serve the soup hot in warmed bowls.

Eggplant, basil, and cannellini soup

SERVES 4

PREPARATION TIME
10 minutes, plus at least
12 hours for soaking beans

COOKING TIME
2 hours

INGREDIENTS

7 oz (200 g) cannellini beans,
soaked overnight in hot
water

6 large shallots, finely
chopped

1 garlic head, cloves
separated and finely
chopped

3 large eggplants, halved
lengthwise

½ bunch of fresh thyme,
chopped

¼ cup good-quality olive oil

3 bunches of fresh basil,
leaves picked and torn, plus
extra, chopped, to serve

½ bottle dry white wine

1½ quarts (liters)
good-quality chicken stock
(home-made is best)

ACCEPTABLE FOR
  RAPID WEIGHT LOSS
and
  WEIGHT CONTROL

Whatever you do, do not skimp on the fresh basil and thyme in this hearty soup. These herbs are the secret to lifting the flavors of the whole dish, and they cut through the heaviness of the cannellini beans and eggplant.

1 Drain the cannellini beans and rinse with cold water. Put into a heavy-based saucepan and cover well with fresh, cold water. Bring to a boil and simmer for about 1½ hours. Drain and set aside.

2 Preheat the oven to 500°F (250°C). Place the eggplant cut-side up on a baking sheet. Using a sharp knife, score the flesh in a crisscross pattern and season with salt. Sprinkle with a little of the garlic and the thyme, and drizzle with half the olive oil. Roast in the oven for 16 minutes or so, until golden. Cool, then peel off skin and discard. Roughly chop the flesh and set aside.

3 Drizzle the remaining olive oil into the bottom of a large, heavy-based saucepan. Add the shallot and sweat with the lid on for a few minutes, until softened but not colored. Add the remaining garlic, cannellini beans, and basil leaves. When the basil has wilted, pour in the wine and stock. Simmer for 5 minutes to infuse the flavor.

4 To finish, take a little of the eggplant flesh and about one-third of the soup and put in a blender or food processor, making sure you include some of the cannellini beans. Blend just enough to form a rough paste—this will thicken the soup. Return to the pan with the rest of the soup and stir through.

5 Serve hot in warmed bowls, with extra basil sprinkled over the top.

SERVES 4

PREPARATION TIME
10 minutes, plus at least
12 hours for soaking beans

COOKING TIME
2½ hours

INGREDIENTS
½ cup dried chickpeas,
soaked overnight in hot
water (or use drained canned
chickpeas instead)

1 tbsp good-quality olive oil

3 oz (100 g) bacon lardons or
cubed pancetta

3 leeks, roughly diced

2 large onions, roughly diced

3 celery sticks, roughly diced

2 carrots, finely diced

1 tbsp chopped fresh thyme
leaves

1¼ cups split red lentils

2½ quarts (liters) water

ACCEPTABLE FOR

WEIGHT CONTROL

Lentil and lardon soup

A rustic and robust soup, and very simple to make. The only time-consuming part is soaking the chickpeas, but even these can be used canned if you wish. Do not add salt to the chickpeas while they are cooking—it only toughens their skins.

1 Drain the chickpeas in a colander and rinse with fresh water. Put into a saucepan and cover well with fresh, cold water. Bring to a boil and simmer for about 1½ hours. Drain and set aside.

2 Drizzle the olive oil into the bottom of a large, heavy-based saucepan over high heat. Add the lardons and fry until browned, then add the leek, onion, celery, carrot, and thyme, and sweat with the lid on for a few minutes to soften and bring out the flavors.

3 Add the lentils and drained chickpeas. Cover with the water and simmer for about 45 minutes, until cooked through.

4 Using a blender or food processor, coarsely blend the soup, then add salt to taste. Return to the pan to warm through.

5 Serve hot in warmed soup bowls.

SERVES 4

PREPARATION TIME
10 minutes

COOKING TIME
20 minutes

INGREDIENTS

3 chicken breasts, about 4 oz (115 g) each, rinsed

Good-quality olive oil

Pinch of salt

4 large carrots, cut into sticks about 1 in (2 cm) long

1 medium bunch celery, cut into sticks about 1 in (2 cm) long

⅓ cup mayonnaise

2 tbsp grainy mustard

4 heads of Little Gem lettuce, leaves separated, rinsed, and patted dry

Vinaigrette (see page 169)

ACCEPTABLE FOR

  RAPID WEIGHT LOSS

and

  WEIGHT CONTROL

Chicken salad with mustard dressing

The crisp lettuce served as a bed in this salad marries well with its creamy chicken topping, while the tangy mustard combines beautifully with the sharpness of the lemon vinaigrette. If you cannot find Little Gem, choose another Cos variety.

1   Preheat the oven to 300°F (150°C). Drizzle the chicken breasts with a little olive oil and season with a pinch of salt. Place on a baking sheet and roast in the oven for 12 minutes. Turn the breasts over and roast on the other side for a further 4–8 minutes, until cooked through. Set aside to cool for 15–20 minutes.

2   Slice the cooled chicken into strips and place in a bowl with the carrot and celery.

3   Add the mayonnaise and mustard, and toss to coat the vegetables.

4   Lay a few lettuce leaves flat on each of 4 serving plates. Divide the chicken salad equally between each serving, spooning over the top of the lettuce.

5   Drizzle each serving with a little vinaigrette and serve.

Leek and asparagus salad

Perfect for fall, the strong, earthy flavors of this salad are provided by the leek, eggplant, and artichoke, and enhanced with fresh herbs and pumpkin seeds. If you are unable to find pumpkinseed oil, simply drizzle with extra olive oil to finish.

SERVES 4

PREPARATION TIME
15 minutes

COOKING TIME
25 minutes

INGREDIENTS
3 bunches of asparagus
(about 1¾ lb/750 g)
Pinch of sea salt
Good-quality olive oil
4 large eggplants, cut into
triangles 1½ in (3 cm) thick
8 leeks, cut into rounds ½ in
(1 cm) thick, rinsed, and
drained in a colander
1 x 14-oz (400-g) can
artichoke hearts, drained,
squeezed, and quartered
2 tbsp chopped fresh dill
2 tbsp chopped fresh chervil
½ cup pumpkin seeds
⅔ cup feta cheese, diced
Pumpkinseed oil to finish

ACCEPTABLE FOR
RAPID WEIGHT LOSS
and
WEIGHT CONTROL

1   Drizzle a small amount of olive oil into a frying pan over a high heat. Sauté the asparagus for 3–4 minutes, or until slightly charred, with the lid on and turning the asparagus frequently. Remove from the pan and set aside to cool.

2   Season the eggplant with a pinch of sea salt and drizzle with a little olive oil (be careful not to use too much). Put in the frying pan and sauté over high heat for 16 minutes, or until a deep roasted color, turning frequently. Remove from the pan and set aside to cool.

3   Now add the leek to the same pan and drizzle a little olive oil onto the leek. Add sea salt to taste, cover with a lid, and sweat over a high heat for 3–4 minutes, or until lightly colored. Remove from the pan and drain in a colander while cooling.

4   Once all the vegetables have cooled completely, cut the asparagus into shorter lengths. Put in a large bowl with the leek and eggplant.

5   Sprinkle on the dill, chervil, and pumpkin seeds. Drizzle a little pumpkinseed oil over the salad, then drop in the feta. To mix, invert the bowl gently, then turn it upright again–do not toss, since this will break everything up, especially the eggplant and feta.

6   Serve at room temperature. (This salad is best served immediately.)

SERVES 4

PREPARATION TIME
10 minutes

COOKING TIME
20 minutes

INGREDIENTS
4 globe artichokes, tops
trimmed and stalks removed

Good-quality olive oil

1 tbsp lemon juice

½ lb (225 g) French beans
(young, green string beans)

3 x 5½-oz (150-g) cans
artichokes in brine, drained,
squeezed and quartered

2 shallots, finely chopped

25 pitted black olives

½ lb (250 g) wild arugula

1 cup freshly grated
Parmesan cheese

FOR THE VINAIGRETTE
1 tsp each lemon juice, white
wine vinegar, Dijon mustard,
and whole-grain mustard
½ cup each olive oil
and sunflower oil

ACCEPTABLE FOR
RAPID WEIGHT LOSS
and

WEIGHT CONTROL

French bean, artichoke, and arugula salad

Redolent of the rich flavors of the Mediterranean, this salad is simple to put together and even easier to eat. Make sure you use the best-quality ingredients you can find—this way, their tastes and textures will speak for themselves.

1 Drizzle the globe artichokes with olive oil. Put 1–2 quarts (liters) water, a pinch of sea salt, and the lemon juice into a deep saucepan and bring to a boil. Add the globe artichokes, cover, reduce heat, and simmer for 16–18 minutes, or until the artichokes are softened. Take the artichokes out of the water with a slotted spoon and allow to cool. Scoop out the tough inner chokes using a spoon.

2 Place the beans in a clean saucepan, cover with water, add a pinch of salt, and boil for 2 minutes. Remove the pan from the heat and tip the beans into a colander, refresh the beans with cold water, then drain well.

3 Mix the beans, globe artichokes, canned artichokes, shallots, and olives in a large bowl and set aside.

4 To make the lemon vinaigrette dressing, whisk all the ingredients together until combined. Add just enough of the vinaigrette to the vegetables to coat lightly, and mix gently by inverting the bowl once, then turning it right side up again—do not toss. (You can store the remainder of the vinaigrette in a screwtop jar in the refrigerator, where it will keep for up to 4 weeks.)

5 Next add the arugula to the salad and mix very gently, by inverting the bowl just once. Sprinkle the Parmesan over the top and serve.

SERVES 4

PREPARATION TIME
15 minutes

COOKING TIME
5 minutes

INGREDIENTS

3 oz (100 g) crisp cooked
bacon

3 oz (100 g) bacon lardons

4 oz (125 g) cherry tomatoes
on the vine, halved

4 oz (120 g) Emmental
cheese, diced

4 oz (120 g) extra fine French
beans (fine green beans),
trimmed

8 black olives, pitted

8 green olives, pitted

8 oz (250 g) mixed salad
leaves such as lollo rosso,
lettuce, dandelion, frisée

Good-quality walnut oil

WALNUT DRESSING

4 tbsp red wine vinegar

3 tbsp sherry vinegar

2 tbsp Dijon mustard

⅔ cup sunflower oil

2½ tbsp good-quality
walnut oil

Pinch of salt

ACCEPTABLE FOR
RAPID WEIGHT LOSS
and
WEIGHT CONTROL

Mélange of salads

Walnut oil imparts a distinctive nutty flavor and aroma here.
Use the best you can find, preferably Lebanese—it is usually
sold in high-end supermarkets and delis. Make sure you avoid
the bland-tasting type often found in health-food stores.

1   Heat the oven to 475°F (225°C). Place the bacon on a baking sheet
and reheat for a few minutes until it becomes crisp again, then drain
on paper towels. (A tip for keeping bacon as flat as possible and
avoiding curled-up edges is to place another baking sheet on top of
the bacon while it is cooking.)

2   In the meantime, brown the lardons in a frying pan or skillet over
high heat. Drain on paper towels.

3   Put the cherry tomatoes in a colander and sprinkle with sea salt.
Leave in the colander to drain off excess juice.

4   To make a simple walnut dressing, put all the ingredients for the
dressing in a glass jar and shake well. (You can store any leftover
dressing for up to 4 weeks in the refrigerator.)

5   In a large bowl, gently mix the bacon, lardons, tomato, cheese,
beans, and olives. Drizzle over a little walnut dressing. In a separate
bowl, drizzle the salad leaves with a little walnut oil. Add salt and
freshly ground black pepper to taste.

6   To serve, alternately layer the bacon mixture and salad leaves in
a serving bowl or on individual plates.

SERVES 4

PREPARATION TIME
15 minutes

COOKING TIME
8 minutes

INGREDIENTS

⅓ cup cumin seed

⅓ cup coriander seed

⅓ cup fennel seed

2 tsp dried red chili pepper
flakes

1 head of garlic, cloves
separated and finely
chopped

Good-quality olive oil

1 cup red wine vinegar

8 oz (250 g) cherry tomatoes,
quartered or halved

7 oz (200 g) cooked flageolet
beans, drained

4 mixed bell peppers,
deseeded and finely chopped

3 red onions, finely chopped

3 oz (100 g) French beans
(fine green beans)

4 fresh red chili peppers,
deseeded and finely chopped

1 tbsp chopped fresh basil

1 tbsp chopped fresh mint

1 lb (500 g) tuna chunks
in oil, drained

ACCEPTABLE FOR
  RAPID WEIGHT LOSS
and
  WEIGHT CONTROL

Flageolet and tuna salad

Dry-roasting the spices used in this salad brings out their full flavor, giving a much better result than buying ready-ground spices. Fresh flageolet beans can be used in place of canned ones, if the season is right and you have the time.

1 Roast the cumin seed, coriander seed, fennel seed, and chili pepper flakes in a dry frying pan or skillet over medium heat for a few minutes, until the aromas of the spices are released. Grind to a powder in a coffee grinder or using a mortar and pestle.

2 Drizzle a little olive oil into a frying pan or skillet over medium heat, and gently sauté the garlic for a few minutes to release the flavor. Add the ground spice, then pour in the red wine vinegar. Transfer everything to a stainless-steel bowl and allow to cool completely. (You can make the dish up to this point, then simply pick up from here closer to serving time if you wish.)

3 Put the cherry tomatoes in a colander and sprinkle liberally with sea salt. Set aside to allow any excess juices to drain, then shake out seeds. (You can omit this step if you wish.)

4 Put the flageolet beans, bell pepper, red onion, French beans, chili peppers, basil, and mint in a bowl. Add the tuna and gently mix through.

5 Pour on the vinegar spice mix, then season with salt to taste and a drizzle of olive oil. Add the cherry tomatoes and mix gently. Serve in a large bowl.

Goat cheese salad

Smoky roast peppers, creamy goat cheese, and peppery arugula—all dressed with a simple lemon vinaigrette enlivened by fresh herbs—combine here to make a light but satisfying salad perfect for a spring or summer lunch.

SERVES 4

PREPARATION TIME
30 minutes, plus 1 hour for defrosting

COOKING TIME
11 minutes

INGREDIENTS
8 oz (250 g) frozen fava beans

4 large yellow peppers, stalks removed

6 tbsp olive oil plus extra for drizzling

4 large tomatoes

1 tbsp chopped fresh basil

1 tbsp chopped fresh mint

Juice of ½ lemon

7 oz (200 g) wild arugula

7 oz (200 g) goat cheese, chopped into ½-in (1-cm) cubes

ACCEPTABLE FOR
RAPID WEIGHT LOSS

and

WEIGHT CONTROL

1 Allow the fava beans to defrost for 1 hour, then peel and put into a large bowl.

2 To roast the peppers, preheat the oven to 475°F (240°C). Remove the stalks and place the whole peppers on a baking sheet. Sprinkle with salt and drizzle with a little olive oil. Roast in the oven for 10 minutes, or until charred and blistered. Remove the peppers from the oven, but do not turn the oven off. Allow the peppers to cool for 20 minutes, then peel off and discard the skin (wear plastic gloves if the peppers are still too hot to handle). Slice the peppers in half, remove the seeds, and cut the flesh into fine strips. Add to the same bowl as the fava beans.

3 To blanch the tomatoes, plunge them into boiling salted water for 20 seconds, then transfer to a bowl of cold water to cool. Peel off and discard the skin, slice the flesh into quarters, and remove the seeds. Slice the flesh into fine strips and add to the bean mixture.

4 Whisk together the 6 tbsp olive oil, a pinch of salt, basil, mint, and lemon juice to make a dressing. Add to the bowl with the arugula and toss gently.

5 Place the goat cheese on a baking sheet and heat through in the hot oven for 1 minute. Top the salad with the warm cheese and serve immediately.

SERVES 4

PREPARATION TIME
15 minutes

COOKING TIME
30 minutes

INGREDIENTS
3 large eggplants, cut into
1-in- (2-cm-) thick triangles

Good-quality olive oil

4 large yellow peppers,
deseeded and cut into large
chunks

4 large red peppers,
deseeded and cut into large
chunks

⅓ cup *herbes de Provence*

3 tbsp garlic purée

2 medium fennel bulbs, cut
into wedges

2 medium red onions, cut
into wedges

2 large zucchini, sliced
lengthwise

ACCEPTABLE FOR
RAPID WEIGHT LOSS
and
WEIGHT CONTROL

Mediterranean oven-roasted vegetables

There is a world of difference between genuine *herbes de Provence* and the pale imitation often found on supermarket shelves. Take the time to search out the best brand you can, even if you have to go to a gourmet food store.

1   Preheat the oven to 500°F (250°C), or the hottest possible setting. Place the eggplant on a baking tray, drizzle with a little olive oil, and lightly sprinkle with a pinch of sea salt. Roast in the oven for 16–19 minutes, or until a rich golden brown. Remove from the oven, place in a bowl, and allow to cool. Reduce the oven temperature to 425°F (220°C).

2   Next, place the peppers on a baking sheet, drizzle with a little olive oil, and sprinkle with a pinch of sea salt, half of the *herbes de Provence*, and the garlic purée. Roast in the oven for 10 minutes. Remove from the oven, place in a colander to strain off juices, and allow to cool. Keep the oven at the same temperature.

3   Finally, place fennel, onion, and zucchini on a baking sheet and drizzle with olive oil, a pinch of salt, and the remaining *herbes de Provence*. Roast in the oven for 8 minutes, or until the fennel is transparent and the onion is golden brown. (If you like, you can roast these vegetables at the same time as the peppers—just remember to take them out after 8 minutes.) Allow to cool.

4   Toss all the vegetables together and serve at room temperature.

SERVES 4

PREPARATION TIME
2 minutes

COOKING TIME
18 minutes

INGREDIENTS
⅔ cup green lentils
⅔ cup red lentils
⅔ cup brown lentils
⅔ cup yellow lentils
Good-quality olive oil

ACCEPTABLE FOR
RAPID WEIGHT LOSS
and
WEIGHT CONTROL

Rainbow lentils

This straightforward but delicious side dish is enhanced by the addition of a little sea salt and olive oil just before serving. As is the case with all legumes, it is important not to add salt to at the start of cooking, since this only toughens the skins.

1 To cook the lentils, put them in separate small saucepans and pour water into each pan so that the lentils are covered with about 2 in (4 cm) of cold water. Bring the green, red, and brown lentils to a boil, then simmer for 10–15 minutes. The yellow lentils will take about 5 minutes to cook and need only be brought to a boil.

2 Test at this point to see whether the lentils are cooked by sampling some with a spoon. There should still be a slight crunch to them, but they should not be hard. This is the point at which you add salt to taste. Cook for a further 3 minutes or so, then strain in a colander and rinse with cold water to cool slightly.

2 To finish, combine all the lentils in one bowl, sprinkle with a touch of sea salt, and stir through so that the different-colored lentils are thoroughly mixed. Drizzle with a little olive oil and serve. This dish can be stored in the refrigerator for up to a few days and simply reheated in the microwave and seasoned before serving.

Braised eggplant with capers

SERVES 4

PREPARATION TIME
15 minutes (note that sauce is made a day ahead)

COOKING TIME
30 minutes

INGREDIENTS
14 oz (400 g) cooked peeled plum tomatoes

Good-quality olive oil

½ head of garlic, cloves separated and finely chopped

2 white onions, finely diced

3 celery sticks, finely diced

½ cup red wine vinegar

3½ oz (100 g) tomato paste

1½ tbsp fructose

7 oz (200 g) green olives, pitted

1 x 5½-oz (150-g) jar capers in brine, rinsed, drained, lightly squeezed, and chopped

1 bunch of fresh flat-leaf parsley, chopped

4 very large or 8 medium eggplants, cut into 1-in (2-cm) dice

ACCEPTABLE FOR
  RAPID WEIGHT LOSS
and
  WEIGHT CONTROL

Another dish with strong flavors reminiscent of sunshine and the Mediterranean, its tomato-based sauce is prepared a day ahead and stored in the refrigerator to allow the piquancy to develop—all the better to contrast with the smoky eggplant.

1   Make the sauce first. Drain the tomatoes in a coarse strainer set over a bowl, pushing down gently to release the juice. Reserve the tomato pulp and strain the juice to remove any seeds.

2   Drizzle a little olive oil into a large, heavy-based saucepan over high heat. Add the garlic, onion, celery, and thyme, and sweat with the lid on for a few minutes, until softened but not colored.

3   Pour in the strained tomato juice, and allow to reduce in volume by two-thirds. Add the red wine vinegar, reserved tomato pulp, tomato paste, and fructose to balance the tomato's acidity. Stir, then reduce the heat and add the olives, capers, and parsley. Check the seasoning and add salt to taste. Remove from the heat. Cool slightly, then transfer to a container to cool overnight in the refrigerator.

4   The next day, preheat the oven to 500°F (250°C) or hottest possible setting. Arrange the eggplant skin-side down on a baking tray. Sprinkle with salt and drizzle with a little olive oil. Roast the eggplant in the oven for about 16 minutes, until a rich golden brown. Allow to cool.

5   Once the eggplant has cooled completely, mix with the tomato sauce. Serve in a large bowl, drizzled with a little olive oil.

SERVES 4

PREPARATION TIME
10 minutes

COOKING TIME
50 minutes

INGREDIENTS
Good-quality olive oil

1 onion, finely chopped

1 red cabbage, quartered, central stalk removed and finely shredded

½ cup red wine vinegar plus a little extra to finish

2 cups red wine

1 cinnamon stick

½ cup fructose

⅔ cup seedless raisins

¾ cup walnuts, chopped

⅔ cup olive oil

1 tbsp *herbes de Provence*

1 bunch of fresh sage leaves, shredded

Good-quality walnut oil (preferably Lebanese)

ACCEPTABLE FOR

WEIGHT CONTROL

Red cabbage in red wine with walnuts and raisins

This tasty salad has its appeal enhanced by the use of red cabbage—just be sure not to overcook it. It is also appealing because it can be made a day ahead, with just a couple of final touches necessary when you are ready to serve.

1 Drizzle a little olive oil into a large, heavy-based saucepan over high heat. Sauté the onion until just softened, then add the cabbage and toss through (or, using pot holders, simply invert the pan with the lid on, then turn right side up). Add salt to taste, red wine vinegar, red wine, and cinnamon stick, and cover the pan with a lid. Allow to simmer gently for about 40 minutes.

2 Add 2 tsp of the *herbes de Provence*, and stir continuously until the cabbage juice has evaporated slightly. Check the seasoning, then add the fructose and raisins. When the cabbage is completely tender, pour into a container and allow to cool completely. (The salad can be made up to this point and stored in the refrigerator until needed.)

3 To finish, remove the cinnamon stick from the cabbage salad, and add the walnuts, sage, remaining 1 tsp *herbes de Provence*, and a small splash of extra red wine vinegar.

4 Serve in a large bowl, drizzled with a little walnut oil.

SERVES 4

PREPARATION TIME
15 minutes

COOKING TIME
35 minutes

INGREDIENTS

4 large red onions, peeled
but left whole

2 tsp olive oil

1 tbsp balsamic vinegar

3 cups good-quality chicken
stock

6 tbsp unsalted butter

¾ cup brown rice

½ white onion, chopped

1 cup freshly grated
Parmesan cheese

½ bunch of fresh thyme,
chopped

½ bunch of fresh rosemary,
chopped

½ bunch of fresh chives,
chopped

½ bunch of fresh tarragon,
chopped

2 tbsp pine nuts

3 tbsp dried cranberries

ACCEPTABLE FOR

WEIGHT CONTROL

Stuffed onions

Roasting the onions before stuffing them brings out their sweetness, which is perfectly offset by the cheesy herb-infused rice stuffing. The pine nuts add crunchiness to the texture of the dish, while the cranberries impart their distinctive tartness.

1   Preheat the oven to 350°F (180°C). Place the whole onions in a ceramic casserole dish and drizzle with the olive oil and balsamic vinegar. Cover with foil and bake in the oven for 30 minutes. Remove from the oven and allow to cool slightly.

2   Meanwhile, prepare the risotto. Heat the chicken stock in a saucepan and keep at a simmer. Melt the butter in a separate, large, heavy-based saucepan over medium heat. Add the rice and chopped onion, and cook, stirring, for a few minutes, until the rice is coated in the butter and the onion has softened. Gradually add the simmering stock a ladleful at a time, stirring continuously, until the rice is swollen and tender. Add the Parmesan, chopped herbs, pine nuts, cranberries, and salt to taste. Stir through and check the seasoning. Keep warm.

3   Using a sharp knife, slice the tops off the cooked onions. Scoop out the flesh from each onion to leave a shell and lid. Fill with the risotto mixture, then top each one with its lid. Reheat slightly and serve on warmed plates.

SERVES 4

PREPARATION TIME
15 minutes

COOKING TIME
20 minutes

INGREDIENTS
Juice of ½ lemon
1 quart (liter) water
8 globe artichokes, tough outer leaves removed and stalks trimmed, halved
7 oz (180 g) goat cheese
Good-quality olive oil
2 tbsp chopped fresh chives
8 oz (250 g) salad greens such as arugula, endive, or frisée, shredded

ACCEPTABLE FOR
RAPID WEIGHT LOSS
and
WEIGHT CONTROL

Artichoke hearts with goat cheese

You could use ready-cooked artichoke hearts for this dish, but fresh ones are much better if they are available. And there is no need to be intimidated by preparing them—it is a quick and simple process, and well worth the effort.

1 Pour the lemon juice into a large, heavy-based saucepan. Add the water, bring to a boil, and carefully drop in the artichokes. Boil for about 5 minutes, then check to see if they are cooked by poking a knife into the heart of an artichoke. Drain and let cool, then scoop out the tough inner choke with a spoon.

2 Preheat the broiler. Crumble the cheese in a bowl and mix with the chives. Add salt and freshly ground black pepper to taste.

3 Sprinkle the cheese on the artichokes and set them in a greased baking dish. Leave under the broiler for about 10 minutes, watching constantly to make sure they do not burn.

4 When the cheese starts to brown, remove from the oven and serve on individual plates on a bed of the salad greens.

Entrées

The dishes that follow
range from quick-and-
easy recipes to hearty
French classics. Rich and
flavorful, every recipe is
compatible with the Diet.
The protein-based recipes
are acceptable for both
plans, but the pasta and
rice dishes (*see pp192–95*)
have a moderate fat
content and are thus
suitable for Weight
Control only.

SERVES 4

PREPARATION TIME
10 minutes

COOKING TIME
28 minutes

INGREDIENTS
1¾ lb (750 g) wild mushrooms
(such as chanterelle, chestnut,
oyster, blue point), sliced
½ medium white onion, finely
chopped
Good-quality olive oil
1 tbsp chopped fresh basil
1 tbsp chopped fresh chives
1 tbsp chopped fresh
tarragon
4 large eggs
½ cup crème fraîche
butter for greasing

ACCEPTABLE FOR
RAPID WEIGHT LOSS
and
WEIGHT CONTROL

Wild mushroom ramekins

There is no need to trek through the woods searching for wild mushrooms these days. Varieties ranging from the chewy, delicate chanterelle to the more robust oyster mushroom are increasingly found in better supermarkets.

1 Lightly grease 4 glass or ceramic ramekins with butter, and preheat the oven to 300°F (150°C).

2 Place the mushroom and onion in a large frying pan over high heat. Drizzle with a little olive oil and add a pinch of salt. Sweat for 2–3 minutes, until the onion has softened but not colored.

3 Pour the mushroom and onion mixture into a colander to drain, then transfer to a bowl. When it has cooled to room temperature, add the basil, chives, and tarragon. Stir through.

4 Break the eggs into a separate bowl. Whisk in the crème fraîche and a pinch of salt. Pour the mushroom and onion mixture into the egg mixture and mix well.

5 Divide the mixture between the 4 ramekins, then set the ramekins in a baking dish filled with water. Carefully place in the oven and cook for 20–25 minutes, until the tops are slightly browned. Serve hot.

SERVES 4

PREPARATION TIME
10 minutes

COOKING TIME
2 hours 45 minutes

INGREDIENTS
10 ripe tomatoes, halved
Good-quality olive oil
1 tsp garlic purée
1 tsp *herbes de Provence*
1 white onion, finely chopped
8 oz (225 g) bacon lardons or
unsmoked bacon, cubed
8 large eggs
2 cups crème fraîche or
heavy cream
2 tbsp tomato paste
1 tbsp chopped fresh chives
4 oz (100 g) Gruyère cheese,
grated

ACCEPTABLE FOR
RAPID WEIGHT LOSS
and
WEIGHT CONTROL

Montignac Gruyère quiche

The roasting and sautéeing carried out before this dish is placed in the oven are important to the finished product. The tomatoes fully develop their flavor and sweetness in tandem with the herbs and garlic, while the onion loses its rawness.

1 Lightly grease a 10-in (26-cm) round ovenproof ceramic dish, and preheat the oven to 300°F (150°C).

2 To make the provençal tomatoes, place the tomato halves face up on a baking tray, drizzle with a little olive oil, then sprinkle with the garlic purée, *herbes de Provence*, and a pinch of salt. Roast in the oven for 1½–2 hours. Remove from the oven and set aside to cool. Do not turn the oven off.

3 Drizzle a little olive oil into a frying pan over high heat. Add the onion and sauté for 2 minutes, until the onion is softened but not colored. Pour into a colander to drain.

4 Add the bacon to the frying pan and sauté over high heat for 3–4 minutes, then put this into the same colander as the onion.

5 Break the eggs into a clean bowl. Whisk in the crème fraîche and tomato paste. Add the chives, bacon, and onion. Mix well.

6 Pour the egg mixture into the buttered ceramic dish, and sprinkle the Gruyère cheese and provençal tomatoes on top—they should float on top of the egg mixture. Bake in the oven for 30–40 minutes, until the top is golden brown. Let cool slightly and serve. This quiche is also delicious served cold.

Salmon and blue cheese quiche

SERVES 4

PREPARATION TIME
15 minutes

COOKING TIME
40 minutes

INGREDIENTS
1 white onion, chopped
Good-quality olive oil
1 cup freshly grated Parmesan cheese
2 tbsp chopped fresh basil
8 large eggs, beaten
1 cup crème fraîche or heavy cream
10 black olives, pitted
10 oz (300 g) smoked salmon, sliced
4 oz (100 g) Roquefort cheese, diced

ACCEPTABLE FOR
RAPID WEIGHT LOSS
and
WEIGHT CONTROL

Smoked salmon and crème fraîche make a classic combination along the same lines as smoked salmon and cream cheese. Add to that duo salty olives and the classic blue cheese Roquefort, and you have a filling, sense-satisfying quiche.

1 Lightly grease a 10-in (26-cm) round ovenproof ceramic dish with butter, and preheat the oven to 300°F (150°C).

2 Drizzle a little olive oil into a frying pan over high heat. Add the onion and sweat for 2–3 minutes, until softened but not colored. Put the onion into a large bowl to cool before adding the Parmesan and basil. Stir through.

3 In a separate bowl, beat together the eggs and crème fraîche. Pour into the onion mixture, add the olives, and mix well before adding the salmon. Stir gently, being careful not to break up the salmon.

4 Pour the egg mixture into the buttered dish. Sprinkle the Roquefort over the mixture—the cheese should float on top. Bake in the oven for 30–40 minutes, or until the top is golden brown. Remove from the oven, cool to room temperature, and serve.

SERVES 4

PREPARATION TIME
20 minutes

COOKING TIME
25 minutes

INGREDIENTS
2 large red bell peppers,
stalk removed

Good-quality olive oil

1 bunch of asparagus, woody
ends trimmed

½ white onion, chopped

12 large eggs

2 tbsp chopped fresh basil
plus extra leaves for garnish

2 tbsp milk

3½ tbsp heavy cream

¾ cup freshly grated
Parmesan cheese

ACCEPTABLE FOR
 RAPID WEIGHT LOSS
and
 WEIGHT CONTROL

Omelet with red peppers and asparagus

This omelet can be made in two ways: as a classic omelet stuffed with the filling of peppers, basil, and asparagus; or like a frittata, egg and filling combined, slow-cooked in a frying pan or baked in the oven at 300°F (150°C) for 20 minutes.

1 Preheat the oven to 425°F (220°C). Place the peppers on a baking sheet, drizzle with a little olive oil, and lightly sprinkle with sea salt. Roast in the oven for 10 minutes, or until the skins are charred and blistered. Allow to cool for 20 minutes, then peel, slice in half, remove seeds, and cut the flesh into fine strips.

2 To prepare the asparagus, blanch in a saucepan of boiling salted water for 2–3 minutes. Drain quickly, then plunge into cold water to refresh. Drain again and chop into shorter lengths.

3 Drizzle a little olive oil into a frying pan over a high heat. Add the onion and sweat for 2–3 minutes, or until soft and opaque. Remove from the heat and allow to cool.

4 Break the eggs into a large bowl. Add the milk, cream, basil, Parmesan, and a pinch of salt. Whisk together until well combined.

5 Drizzle a little olive oil into a clean, large frying pan and pour in the egg mixture (you can make individual omelets if you wish). Cook over low to medium heat for 15–20 minutes, checking often to make sure the bottom does not burn. When the omelet has almost set, sprinkle the peppers, asparagus, and onion over one half, fold the omelet over the top, and slide out of the pan onto a serving plate. Slice into 4 pieces, garnish with the extra basil, and serve.

SERVES 4

PREPARATION TIME
10 minutes

COOKING TIME
6–8 minutes

INGREDIENTS
Grated zest and juice of
2 lemons

½ cup olive oil

Pinch of salt

1 lb (400 g) whole-wheat
pasta, such as spaghetti

10 oz (300 g) canned tuna,
drained in a colander

7 oz (200 g) canned artichoke
hearts, drained, squeezed,
and quartered

2–2½ oz (60–70 g) sun-dried
tomatoes, shredded

15 black olives, pitted

2 oz (60 g) capers (rinsed
and squeezed if in brine)

½ cup fresh flat-leaf parsley,
chopped

ACCEPTABLE FOR

WEIGHT CONTROL

Pasta with tuna and artichokes

The key to this dish is cooking the pasta after you have all the other elements prepared and ready to go. Once the pasta is cooked, you need to move quickly. The lemon mixture is added first so that its flavor is absorbed into the hot pasta.

1   Mix the lemon zest and juice, olive oil, and pinch of salt in a bowl.

2   Bring a large saucepan of salted water to a boil. Add the pasta to the pan and cook 6–8 minutes, until *al dente*—do not overcook. Drain in a colander, but keep just a little of the cooking water back. Quickly return the pasta to the pan with the cooking water, and season with salt and freshly ground black pepper.

3   Pour in the lemon and oil mixture and stir through, taking care not to break the pasta. Add the tuna, artichokes, sun-dried tomatoes, olives, capers, and parsley. Stir through and serve immediately in a large, shallow bowl.

SERVES 4

PREPARATION TIME
5 minutes

COOKING TIME
30 minutes

INGREDIENTS

1 cup long-grain
brown rice

1 cup basmati rice

½ cup wild rice

Good-quality olive oil

3 white onions, finely
chopped

2 cups balsamic vinegar

ACCEPTABLE FOR

WEIGHT CONTROL

Tricolor rice

This is an appetizing and slightly different way to serve rice, with its sticky, caramelized onions and blending of textures and flavors in the rice itself. It is also just as good reheated as it is served fresh from the pan the first time around.

1 Put each type of rice into its own heavy-based saucepan. Gently pour enough cold water into each pot to cover the rice by 2½ in (5 cm). Cover and bring to a boil, then continue cooking at a steady but not too vigorous boil for 16–20 minutes. Put all the rice into a colander to drain off any liquid, then cool with cold running water. Allow to drain thoroughly once again.

2 Drizzle a little olive oil into a frying pan or wok over high heat. Add the onion and fry for a few minutes, until golden. Pour in the balsamic vinegar and reduce until the onion is dark and sticky.

3 Add the rice to the pan or wok, season with salt to taste, and stir through. The rice is then ready to use. (If you are not serving the rice right away, it can be refrigerated and reheated in either a microwave or a wok.) Serve in a bowl.

SERVES 4

PREPARATION TIME
15 minutes

COOKING TIME
35 minutes

INGREDIENTS
Good-quality of olive oil

3 garlic cloves, finely chopped

1 onion, finely chopped

1 tbsp chopped fresh thyme

4 red bell peppers, cut into ½-in (1-cm) dice

4 yellow bell peppers, cut into ½-in (1-cm) dice

1 large eggplant, cut into ½-in (1-cm) dice

2 zucchini, cut into ½-in (1-cm) dice

400 g (14 oz) tomato sauce

1 or 2 fresh bay leaves

10 oz (300 g) whole-wheat linguini

Dash of sherry vinegar

Dash of red wine vinegar

1 tbsp whole-grain mustard

2 tbsp chopped fresh flat-leaf parsley

4 oz (120 g) cherry tomatoes, halved and drained in a colander

1 cup grated Parmesan cheese

ACCEPTABLE FOR

WEIGHT CONTROL

Linguini with ratatouille

Make sure you have all your vegetables chopped and ready first when preparing this dish. It helps with the timing of putting everything together at the end, since this pasta and its flavor-filled ratatouille need to be served hot.

1 To make the ratatouille, pour a glug of olive oil into a heavy-based saucepan over high heat. When the oil is hot, add the garlic, onion, and thyme, and sauté briskly. Now add the peppers. Sweat with the lid on for 5 minutes before adding the eggplant and zucchini. Add salt to taste. Add the tomato sauce and bay leaf, reduce the heat, and simmer gently for 30 minutes.

2 Bring a large saucepan of salted water to a boil. Add the linguine and cook for 6–8 minutes, until *al dente*. Drain in a colander, reserving just a little of the cooking water.

3 Quickly return the pasta to the pan with the reserved cooking water and, while it is still hot, drizzle in a little olive oil and add the sherry vinegar, red wine vinegar, and mustard. Stir through and add salt to taste.

4 Now quickly stir the parsley and cherry tomato into the ratatouille, and discard the bay leaf.

5 To serve, take 4 serving bowls and, using two spoons, put a layer of pasta in the bottom of each bowl. Spoon on some ratatouille. Repeat until all the pasta and ratatouille are used. Serve immediately, sprinkled with Parmesan and drizzled with olive oil.

SERVES 4

PREPARATION TIME
10 minutes

COOKING TIME
6–8 minutes

INGREDIENTS

Juice of 2 lemons

1 cup olive oil

10 oz (300 g) whole-wheat
penne

2 oz (60 g) sun-dried
tomatoes, shredded

5 cloves garlic, finely
chopped

20 black olives, pitted

20 green olives, pitted

3–4 tbsp capers in brine,
rinsed, drained, and
squeezed

½ bunch of fresh flat-leaf
parsley, chopped

Pinch of chili pepper flakes
(optional)

ACCEPTABLE FOR

WEIGHT CONTROL

Penne with capers and olives

Another dish with a strong *provençal* influence, this fresh-tasting pasta is packed with clean, strong flavors that do not overwhelm. The chili pepper flakes add a little kick if this is something you enjoy, but are readily omitted if you prefer.

1   Combine the lemon juice, a pinch of salt, and olive oil in a bowl.

2   Bring a large saucepan of salted water to a boil. Add the penne and cook for 6–8 minutes, until *al dente*. Drain in a colander, keeping back just a little of the cooking water.

3   Quickly return the penne to the pan with the reserved cooking water, and season with salt and freshly ground black pepper to taste. Stir in the lemon-and-oil mixture, then add the sun-dried tomato, garlic, olives, capers, parsley, and chili pepper flakes, if using. Stir through and serve immediately in warmed pasta bowls.

Salmon provençale

This dish could hardly be easier to make—succulent salmon steaks topped with a fresh herb and tomato salsa with the zing of lemon and balsamic vinegar. A little chopping, a little whisking, a touch of cooking, and it is ready to go.

SERVES 4

PREPARATION TIME
10 minutes

COOKING TIME
12 minutes

INGREDIENTS
3 large tomatoes
3 shallots, roughly chopped
1 tbsp roughly chopped fresh chervil
1 tbsp roughly chopped fresh basil
1 tbsp roughly chopped fresh tarragon
1 tbsp roughly chopped fresh chives
Juice of ½ lemon
1½ tbsp balsamic vinegar
2 tbsp olive oil plus extra for drizzling
4 boneless salmon steaks, about 5 oz (150 g) each
Pinch of salt

ACCEPTABLE FOR
RAPID WEIGHT LOSS
and
WEIGHT CONTROL

1   Preheat the oven to 300°F (150°C).

2   Blanch the tomatoes by plunging them into a pan of boiling salted water for 1 minute, then plunging into cold water for 1 minute. Drain the tomatoes and peel off and discard the skin. Cut the tomatoes into quarters, remove the core (including seeds), and dice the flesh.

3   Put the tomatoes in a bowl with the shallot, chervil, basil, tarragon, and chives. Whisk together the lemon juice, balsamic vinegar, and 2 tbsp olive oil. Add to the tomato mixture and toss through.

4   Season the salmon with a pinch of salt and drizzle with a little extra olive oil. Heat a large frying pan over high heat, and sear the steaks for 30 seconds on each side. Transfer the salmon to a baking dish and bake in the oven for 12 minutes, until cooked through.

5   To serve, drain the salmon on paper towels to absorb any excess oil, then place a steak on each of 4 plates. Spoon 1–2 tbsp or so of the tomato mixture over each salmon steak and serve immediately.

SERVES 4

PREPARATION TIME
20 minutes

COOKING TIME
30 minutes

INGREDIENTS
12 cherry tomatoes
8 thin slices pancetta
Good-quality olive oil
4 cod fillets, skin on, about
4 oz (120 g) each
Small pat of butter
½ cup Puy lentils, cooked
(see p176)
Juice of ½ lemon
3 oz (100 g) fresh spinach
Pinch of ground nutmeg

FRESH TOMATO SAUCE
1 onion, chopped
3 celery sticks
2 tsp olive oil
1 lb (500 g) ripe tomatoes,
chopped
2 tbsp each chopped fresh
basil and tarragon
8 oz (250 g) canned peeled
tomatoes, drained
Juice of 1 lemon
¼ cup white wine vinegar

ACCEPTABLE FOR
RAPID WEIGHT LOSS
and
WEIGHT CONTROL

Cod on a bed of lentils

This is a dish of layers, each one complementing the others.
If cod is unavailable, choose another delicate white fish fillet.
Baking the pancetta between two baking sheets helps it to stay
nice and flat, rather than curling up during cooking.

1 To make the tomato sauce, sweat the onion and celery in the olive
oil in a heavy-based saucepan over high heat for a few minutes,
until softened. Reduce the heat to medium, and add the fresh
tomatoes, basil, and tarragon. Cook until the tomatoes have broken
up, then pour in the canned tomatoes, lemon juice, and white wine
vinegar. Simmer gently until a thick sauce has formed. Keep warm.

2 Preheat the oven to 475°F (225°C). Place the cherry tomatoes on a
baking sheet. Sprinkle with salt and drizzle with a little olive oil. Lay
the pancetta on another baking sheet, then place a tray of the same
size on top. Quickly roast the cherry tomatoes in the oven, until the
skins just start to split. Remove from the oven and put in the double
tray of pancetta. Bake for 6 minutes, until the pancetta is crispy.

3 Season the cod with salt. Drizzle a little olive oil into a frying pan
over medium heat, then add a pat of butter. Cook the fish skin-side
up, until the bottom is golden brown.

4 Sweat the lentils in a drizzle of olive oil in a covered heavy-based
saucepan over high heat for about 3 minutes. Add the lemon juice,
spinach, and nutmeg. Cook until the spinach has just wilted.

5 Place a small pile of spinach and lentils on each of 4 plates. Put
a cod fillet on each serving. Crisscross the pancetta over the top.
Drizzle some fresh tomato sauce around the fish, and serve
immediately.

Grilled sea bass with tapenade

SERVES 4

PREPARATION TIME
15 minutes, plus 2 hours
for marinating

COOKING TIME
12–20 minutes

INGREDIENTS
4 sea bass steaks, skin on,
about 4 oz (120 g) each
1 tbsp each chopped fresh
chervil, basil, and tarragon

FOR THE MARINADE
3 tbsp ground coriander
3 garlic cloves, chopped
Juice of 1 lemon
¼ cup olive oil

FOR THE TAPENADE
7 oz (200 g) black olives,
pitted
2 oz (60 g) capers in brine
1 x 1-oz (30-g) can desalted
anchovies, drained
3 garlic cloves
2 tbsp chopped fresh parsley
Juice of ½ lemon
¼ cup olive oil

ACCEPTABLE FOR
RAPID WEIGHT LOSS
and
WEIGHT CONTROL

There are two basic options when it comes to grilling the fish, depending on the weather and your inclination. You can cook it on an outdoor grill, or you can choose to cook it under a broiler—you could even use a cast-iron griddle.

1   Rinse and trim the fish. Slash the skin of each fish steak to prevent the fish from curling up during cooking. Combine the ingredients for the marinade. Lay the fish in a glass or ceramic dish, pour on the marinade, and leave to marinate in the refrigerator for a couple of hours.

2   To prepare the tapenade, first drain, rinse, and squeeze out excess liquid from the capers. Blend or process all the tapenade ingredients to a paste. Keep in a ramekin or small serving dish until needed.

3   If you are using a barbecue grill, season the fish with salt to taste, then drizzle with a little olive oil. When the grill is hot, cook the fish for 10 minutes, then turn over and cook on the other side for 10 minutes, until golden on both sides. If you are using a broiler, place the fish in a lightly oiled pan, season with salt to taste, and cook for about 6 minutes on each side.

4   When the fish is cooked, take some of the fresh tapenade and brush over the surface of the fish. Work the tapenade into the flesh slightly.

5   To serve, place a fish steak on each of 4 serving plates. Drizzle a little olive oil over the fish, and drop a tablespoon or so of tapenade on top. Sprinkle on the herbs and serve immediately.

Grilled tuna with Mediterranean marinade

SERVES 4

PREPARATION TIME
5 minutes, plus 4 hours for marinating

COOKING TIME
12 minutes

INGREDIENTS
4 fresh red tuna or salmon fillets, about ½ lb (250 g) each

Juice of 1½ lemons

3 tbsp olive oil

MEDITERRANEAN MARINADE
3 garlic cloves, crushed

2 tsp ground cumin

2 tsp grated fresh ginger

1 tsp saffron threads or ground coriander

ACCEPTABLE FOR

RAPID WEIGHT LOSS

and

WEIGHT CONTROL

Fresh tuna is an excellent fish to grill, especially as it is done here. After soaking up a simple marinade of lemon and olive oil, the fillets are coated with a spicy "dry" rub before being finished on the barbecue grill or under the broiler.

1   Set the fish in a glass or ceramic bowl with the lemon juice and olive oil, and leave to marinate in the refrigerator for a few hours.

2   To make the marinade, mix the garlic with the cumin. Add the ginger and season with salt and freshly ground black pepper to taste. Mix together, then add the saffron and stir through.

3   Dip each fish fillet in the marinade mixture (if necessary, wet the fish well first to make the coating stick). Cook the fish for 12 minutes on a hot barbecue grill or under the broiler, turning after about 8 minutes so that it cooks evenly on both sides.

SERVES 4

PREPARATION TIME
15 minutes

COOKING TIME
15 minutes

INGREDIENTS
1 tbsp fennel seed

2 large fennel bulbs,
including greenery

Good-quality olive oil

16 large shrimp, peeled and
deveined, but with the heads
left on

Squeeze of lemon juice

½ cup pastis or Pernod

2 tbsp cold unsalted butter,
cubed

ACCEPTABLE FOR

RAPID WEIGHT LOSS

and

WEIGHT CONTROL

Shrimp à la pastis

Pastis, a licorice-flavored apéritif akin to Pernod, is extremely popular in southern France. Fennel, of course, has a gentle aniselike flavor, which is enhanced here by using freshly ground fennel seed, rather than store-bought ground fennel.

1   Roast the fennel seed in a dry frying pan (no oil) over high heat for a few minutes, to release the flavor. Remove from the heat and grind to a fine powder using a mortar and pestle.

2   Trim the fennel bulb, reserving the greenery at the top for later use. Halve the bulb and cut off the root at an angle. Discard the root and chop the bulb as finely as possible.

3   Drizzle a little olive oil into a large frying pan over high heat. Season the shrimp with a little salt, and lightly dust with the fennel seed powder. Cook the shrimp in the pan for a few minutes, then remove to a plate.

4   Add the chopped fennel bulb to the same pan, and cook until softened, then return the shrimp to the pan and squeeze in the lemon juice. Pour in the pastis and flambé the shrimp until the alcohol has evaporated.

5   Spoon the fennel and shrimp into warmed serving bowls. Gently reduce the heat under the pan, and add the cream to the cooking liquid. Whisk in the butter until combined (it is important that the butter be cold). Quickly chop a little of the fennel greenery and sprinkle into the sauce. Pour the sauce over the shrimp and serve immediately.

Soupe d'Atlantique

SERVES 4

PREPARATION TIME
10 minutes

COOKING TIME
25 minutes

INGREDIENTS
3 shallots, finely chopped

1 lb (500 g) mussels, scrubbed and beards removed

2 tsp olive oil

1¾ cups dry white wine

2 cups good-quality fish stock

2 cups good-quality herb or white vegetable stock (see method)

1 star anise

2 pints (1 liter) heavy cream

2 tbsp chopped fresh dill

ACCEPTABLE FOR

RAPID WEIGHT LOSS

and

WEIGHT CONTROL

In this hearty, satisfying soup, the seafood lies like a treasure trove at the bottom of the bowls. It is easy enough to make your own herb stock, but if you choose not to, be sure to buy a good-quality stock that does not contain carrots.

1 Heat a large, heavy-based saucepan over medium heat. Add the shallot, mussels, and olive oil. Cook until the mussels begin to open, then add the white wine. Continue cooking until the mussels cook completely. Remove from the pan and set aside; discard any mussels that do not open. Strain the mussel liquid and return to the pan.

2 Add the fish stock, herb stock, and star anise. Bring to a boil and reduce in volume by half. Whisk in the cream and continue reducing until the stock begins to thicken. Check the seasoning and add salt to taste if necessary. Reduce the heat and keep warm.

3 Arrange all the seafood in 4 shallow serving bowls, dividing the selection equally among each dish. Bring the soup back to a boil. Ladle the hot soup over the contents of the bowls—this will poach the seafood until it is cooked. Sprinkle over the dill and serve.

HERB STOCK Melt 1 tbsp butter in a stockpot or saucepan over a medium heat. Add 1 chopped leek, 2 chopped onions, ½ chopped celery stick, and ½ head of chopped garlic. Sweat for 5–6 minutes, until softened but not colored. Add 2 sprigs of fresh thyme, 1 parsley stalk, 1 tsp coriander seed, ½ bottle dry white wine, and a good pinch of salt. Cover with 2 cups cold water. Bring to a vigorous boil, then add 1 bunch each of fresh sage, basil, cilantro, and dill. Add more salt if needed, to bring out the full flavor. Simmer gently for 30 minutes. Strain through a fine sieve, discarding the vegetables and herbs. (The stock can be kept in the refrigerator for several days, or frozen and defrosted as needed.)

SERVES 4

PREPARATION TIME
10 minutes

COOKING TIME
8 minutes

INGREDIENTS
4 fresh cod or other firm
white fish fillets, about 6 oz
(180 g) each, cut into large
cubes

8 small slices Parma ham
or prosciutto

1 tbsp olive oil

1 lb (450 g) savoy cabbage
or kale, outer leaves and
hard core removed, shredded

1 tsp cumin or fennel seed

1 tbsp chopped fresh thyme
or parsley, plus extra to serve

1 tbsp wine vinegar

ACCEPTABLE FOR
RAPID WEIGHT LOSS
and
WEIGHT CONTROL

Fresh cod and Parma ham rolls

Wrapping the Parma ham around the cod keeps the fish firmly in place as it cooks, as the ham forms a sort of edible shrink-wrapping. The cod and Parma ham rolls contrast well with the strong flavor of the spiced cabbage.

1 Season the cod with salt and pepper to taste (be careful with the salt, since Parma ham can be very salty on its own). Divide into 8 portions and wrap in the ham slices, placing the cubes along one short end of the ham and rolling up lengthwise.

2 Heat 1 tbsp olive oil in a frying pan over high heat, and cook the wrapped fish for about 4 minutes on each side, until the ham is brown and the fish is cooked.

3 Meanwhile, gently steam the cabbage for about 5 minutes. Do not overcook it, since it needs to keep its color, and do not boil.

4 Mix the cabbage with the cumin seed, 1 tbsp thyme, vinegar, and a drizzle of olive oil. Season with salt and freshly ground black pepper to taste.

5 Make a bed of the cabbage on a serving dish, arrange the cod rolls on top, and sprinkle with the extra thyme. Serve immediately.

SERVES 4

PREPARATION TIME
10 minutes

COOKING TIME
50 minutes

INGREDIENTS

1 bunch of fresh tarragon, chopped, plus extra for garnish

½ bunch of fresh basil, chopped

½ bunch of fresh chives, chopped

½ bunch of fresh basil, chopped

4 boneless chicken breasts with skin on, about 4 oz (120 g) each

3 heads of garlic, cloves separated but unpeeled

4 cups milk

4 tsp olive oil

2½ pints (1.2 liters) soy cream

1½ tbsp paprika

ACCEPTABLE FOR
RAPID WEIGHT LOSS
and
WEIGHT CONTROL

Chicken breast in creamy garlic sauce

Slow-roasting whole garlic cloves in milk not only softens them, but also brings out the sweetness and flavor, and rids them of any sharpness. The resulting sauce makes a creamy complement to the herb-packed grilled chicken.

1 Preheat the oven to 325°F (160°C). Mix together the tarragon, basil, chives, and chervil. Using a teaspoon, push the herbs under the skin of the chicken breasts. Reserve on a tray in the refrigerator covered with plastic wrap.

2 Blanch the garlic in a saucepan of boiling water for a minute or so. Discard the water and place the garlic in a small ceramic oven dish, and cover with a little fresh water and the milk, and then the olive oil. Cover with foil and bake in the oven for 40 minutes, until the garlic is soft. Strain the garlic-infused milk into a small, heavy-based saucepan. Squeeze the garlic cloves to extract the pulp, adding to the milk. Bring to a gentle simmer, whisking. Keep warm.

3 Heat a grill pan or griddle over medium heat. Season the chicken breasts with freshly ground black pepper and salt to taste, and grill for 7 minutes on each side. When cooked, bring the garlic sauce back to a simmer and whisk in the soy cream and paprika. Do not boil, since this will curdle the sauce.

4 To serve, cut each chicken in half on the diagonal. Pour some garlic sauce onto the bottom of each of 4 warmed serving plates. Open the chicken out slightly and set on top of the sauce, adding a few extra sprigs of fresh tarragon. Serve immediately.

Rustic duck à l'orange

SERVES 4

PREPARATION TIME
20 minutes

COOKING TIME
1 hour 15 minutes

INGREDIENTS

2 ducks, about 3 lb 3 oz
(1.5 kg) each

½ head of garlic, cloves
separated and finely
chopped

½ bunch of fresh thyme,
chopped, plus extra for
stuffing and garnish

Zest of 2 oranges, cut into
fine strips

1 orange, halved, plus a few
slices for garnish

Olive oil

2 tbsp chopped fresh parsley

ORANGE SAUCE

1 tsp butter

6 shallots, finely chopped

Zest of 2 oranges, cut into
very fine strips

2 tbsp fructose

4 tbsp malt vinegar

4 cups veal stock

2 tbsp orange juice

Juice of ½ lemon

ACCEPTABLE FOR
RAPID WEIGHT LOSS
and
WEIGHT CONTROL

A rustic variation of a classic French dish, this dish need not be daunting at all—it all comes together very easily. Baste the duck frequently while it is cooking. This keeps the dark, red meat of the bird moist and turns the skin a rich, crisp gold.

1 Preheat the oven to 400°F (200°C). Check that the duck has been cleaned inside, and remove the wishbones using a boning knife. Mix together the garlic, chopped thyme, and orange zest. Lift up the skin of each duck and smear the garlic mixture under the breast and between the legs using a teaspoon. Season the duck with salt to taste, and rub some of the garlic mixture over the outside of each one. Place an orange half inside the cavity of each duck, together with a large sprig of extra thyme. Tie up using kitchen twine, closing the cavities and bringing the legs together.

2 Place the ducks on their sides in a baking pan. Drizzle very lightly with olive oil and place in the oven to roast. After 18 minutes, turn onto their other sides and roast for a further 18 minutes. Lastly, turn onto their backs and roast for 30 minutes. Baste continually as they roast so that they turn a rich golden brown. When cooked, remove from the oven and drain on a wire rack set over a tray. Keep warm.

3 Meanwhile, prepare the sauce. Heat a saucepan over medium heat. Add the butter, shallot, and orange zest. When hot and bubbling, sprinkle in the fructose and allow to caramelize slightly. Add the malt vinegar, stock, and orange juice. Bring the sauce to a simmer. Reduce in volume by about a third, until it begins to thicken. Finish with the lemon juice and a pinch of salt. Keep hot until needed.

4 Carve the duck and arrange on 4 warmed plates. Lay some orange slices over the top, sprinkle on the parsley, and drizzle with sauce.

Chicken with figs

Baking this dish in wine helps to keep the chicken moist, while bringing out the subtle flavors of the other ingredients. The juicy figs and fresh shallots complement one another, giving this chicken dish just the right balance of sweet and savory.

SERVES 4

PREPARATION TIME
15 minutes

COOKING TIME
25 minutes

INGREDIENTS
4 skinless chicken breasts, about ¼ lb (120 g) each

8 fresh figs, sliced, plus 4 extra, whole, for garnish

Good-quality olive oil

3 large shallots, sliced

½ cup dry white wine

¾ cup cold butter, cubed

1–2 tsp fructose

ACCEPTABLE FOR
RAPID WEIGHT LOSS

and

WEIGHT CONTROL

1 Preheat the oven to 350°F (180°C), and lightly butter an ovenproof ceramic dish large enough to hold the chicken.

2 Rinse the chicken breasts and pat dry with paper towels. Place each breast between 2 pieces of plastic wrap. Using a rolling pin, roll over each breast to flatten. Remove the top piece of plastic wrap.

3 Place a few slices of fig down the center of each chicken breast, and fold the chicken over to make a parcel. Drizzle with a little olive oil and a pinch of salt. Secure each parcel with a toothpick, and lay in the bottom of the ovenproof dish.

4 Scatter in the shallot, and pour in the white wine and a splash of water. Cover with foil, and bake in the oven for 20 minutes. Remove the chicken from the dish and keep warm. Whisk the butter into the cooking juices until it has emulsified into a sauce. Keep warm.

5 For the garnish, increase the oven temperature to 400°F (200°C). Take the extra 4 figs and cut a cross in the top of each one. Pinch the bottom of each fig to open up the top, then place on a baking sheet. Sprinkle with the fructose and drizzle with a little olive oil. Roast in the oven for 5 minutes.

6 To serve, place a chicken parcel on each of 4 serving plates. Spoon the sauce over the parcels, and garnish each plate with a roasted whole fig. Serve immediately.

Coq au vin

SERVES 4

PREPARATION TIME
15 minutes

COOKING TIME
50 minutes

INGREDIENTS

1 whole chicken, about 2¼ lb (1 kg), jointed (you can ask the butcher to do this)

1 bottle red wine (or enough to cover chicken)

Pinch of salt

Good-quality olive oil

6 oz (150 g) pearl onions, soaked in hot water until softened, then peeled

1 tbsp butter

1 tbsp finely chopped fresh thyme leaves

1 bay leaf (fresh is best)

2 cups beef stock

4 oz (125 g) lardons or unsmoked bacon, chopped

6 oz (150 g) mushrooms, sliced

2 tbsp chopped fresh parsley

ACCEPTABLE FOR

RAPID WEIGHT LOSS

and

WEIGHT CONTROL

Coq au vin is such a classic it can sometimes be overlooked, but familiarity should not breed contempt. And although it is not a "one-pot" dish, its preparation is not as complicated as it might seem at first glance, and the results are well worth it.

1 Place the chicken pieces in a large ceramic dish, pour in the red wine, and cover. Marinate in the refrigerator for at least 1 hour.

2 Transfer the chicken to a clean dish or plate, reserving the marinade. Season the chicken with a pinch of salt and drizzle of olive oil. Heat a large, heavy-based saucepan over a high heat, add the chicken, and cook for 6–7 minutes, turning until golden on all sides.

3 Remove the chicken from the pan and drain on paper towels. Pour any cooking juices out of the pan and wipe the pan clean.

4 Put the pearl onions in a frying pan, cover with water, and add the butter. Boil off the liquid and cook the onions until golden brown.

5 Put the onions, thyme, and bay leaf into the clean saucepan, then add the reserved wine marinade and the stock. Return the chicken to the pan and poach over medium heat for about 40 minutes, until cooked through. Remove the chicken from the pan and keep warm. Bring the cooking liquid to a boil and reduce by about one-third.

6 Meanwhile, fry the lardons in a frying pan over high heat for 2–3 minutes until crispy. Remove to a plate, then sauté the mushroom in the same pan for 2 minutes.

7 Pour the reduced sauce over the chicken. Add the onions, lardons, and mushroom, and sprinkle over the parsley. Serve immediately.

Turkey brochettes with vegetables à la provençal

This dish displays its *provençal* roots in the tomato, eggplant, and sweet pepper used in the sauce. Strong, earthy flavors are trademarks of *provençal* cuisine, and the emphasis is on using the best possible ingredients for the best possible result.

SERVES 4

PREPARATION TIME
10 minutes

COOKING TIME
15 minutes

INGREDIENTS

4 turkey cutlets, about 4 oz (120 g) each, cut into thick slices

3 tbsp olive oil

1 eggplant, cut into rounds ½ in (1 cm) thick

1 yellow bell pepper, seeded and cut into strips

1 tbsp dry white wine

14 oz (400 g) canned peeled tomatoes

1½ tbsp fresh thyme leaves

1 or 2 bay leaves (fresh is best)

ACCEPTABLE FOR

RAPID WEIGHT LOSS

and

WEIGHT CONTROL

1 Divide the turkey into 4 equal portions and thread the pieces onto 4 skewers. (If using wooden or bamboo skewers, these will need to be soaked in water for at least 15 minutes before using.)

2 Heat the olive oil in a large frying pan over high heat, and cook the brochettes for 5 minutes, turning frequently to brown all sides. Remove from the pan and set aside, but do not remove the meat from the skewers.

3 Add the eggplant and pepper to the same pan, and cook for a few minutes, stirring occasionally, until the vegetables are softened and the eggplant is starting to brown.

4 Add the wine, tomato, thyme, and bay leaf. Reduce the heat to medium and cook for 5 minutes, stirring occasionally.

5 Return the turkey brochettes to the pan and cook for a further 3 minutes. Add salt and freshly ground black pepper to taste, and discard the bay leaf.

6 To serve, place the turkey brochettes on a serving platter, still on their skewers, and either cover them with the vegetable sauce or put it in heaps beside them. Serve immediately.

Braised lamb shanks

SERVES 4

PREPARATION TIME
5 minutes, plus 24 hours
for marinating

COOKING TIME
2 hours 15 minutes

INGREDIENTS
4 lamb shanks, about 1 lb
(400 g) each
1 bottle red wine plus
½ bottle extra (optional)
1 onion, chopped
1 bunch of fresh thyme
leaves
1 bay leaf
1.5 quarts (liters) veal or beef
stock

ACCEPTABLE FOR

RAPID WEIGHT LOSS

and

WEIGHT CONTROL

Lamb shanks benefit greatly from long, slow cooking. The meat becomes sweeter, and will be so tender it nearly falls off the bone. And it truly does improve the dish to marinate the shanks for as long as possible, so try not to skimp on this.

1 Put the lamb shanks into a large ceramic dish. Pour in the wine and marinate in the refrigerator for at least 24 hours. Drain the shanks, reserving the marinade.

2 Seal the shanks in a frying pan over medium heat, browning on all sides. Transfer to a large heavy-based saucepan. Add the onion, and sweat for a couple of minutes, until the onion has softened.

3 Pour in the reserved marinade, splash in the extra wine, if using, and add the thyme and bay leaf. Pour in the stock, cover with a lid, and cook for 2 hours over medium heat, until tender.

4 Remove the lamb from the pan and set on a plate. Bring the cooking liquid to a boil and reduce in volume by a third. Return the lamb to the pan, skim off any fat, and serve.

North African lamb stew

SERVES 4

PREPARATION TIME
15 minutes

COOKING TIME
1½ hours

INGREDIENTS
2 tbsp coriander seed
2 tbsp cumin seed
2 tbsp fennel seed
1 tsp chili pepper flakes
Good-quality olive oil
2 lb (1 kg) diced lamb, trimmed of fat or gristle
3 onions, sliced
1 tbsp chopped fresh ginger root
1 tsp paprika
½ cup tomato sauce
½ cup veal or beef stock
⅔ cup cooked chickpeas
3 eggplants, diced
4 large tomatoes
1 tbsp chopped fresh cilantro

ACCEPTABLE FOR
RAPID WEIGHT LOSS
and
WEIGHT CONTROL

This slow-cooked dish is actually a braise—this is where the meat is cooked very slowly, but in very little liquid. Not only is this a common method of cooking meat in North Africa, but the signature flavors are also typical of its cuisines.

1 Roast the coriander seed, cumin seed, fennel seed, and chili pepper flakes in a dry frying pan over medium heat for a few minutes to release the flavors. Grind to a powder using a mortar and pestle.

2 Season the lamb with a little salt. Drizzle a little olive oil into a large, heavy-based saucepan over medium heat, and brown the meat on all sides. Drain the lamb in a colander with a bowl underneath. Add the onion to the same pan, and cook until soft and golden in color. Transfer to the colander with the lamb. Finally, add the ginger to the pan, let it sizzle for a couple of minutes, then put the contents of the colander and the bowl beneath it back into the pan. Add the ground spices, paprika, salt to taste, tomato sauce, and stock. Braise gently for 1½ hours, then add the chickpeas and stir through.

3 Toward the end of the cooking time, preheat the oven to 475°F (225°C), or the hottest possible setting. Place the eggplant on a baking sheet, drizzle with a little olive oil, and sprinkle with a pinch of sea salt. Roast in the oven for 16 minutes, or until golden brown.

4 To blanch the tomatoes, plunge into boiling water for 1 minute, then refresh in cold water for another minute. Peel, quarter, and remove the seeds. Cut the flesh into strips. Drain any juices into the lamb.

5 When the stew is cooked, add the coriander. Pour the stew into a ceramic serving dish, and drizzle with a little olive oil. Sprinkle the eggplant and tomato strips over the top. Serve.

Lamb provençal

Tomato and basil are used in their customary pairing in this recipe, but with a twist. Tomato sauce is used in the base for the stew, while sweet and juicy oven-roasted cherry tomatoes and fresh basil are used to finish it all off.

SERVES 4

PREPARATION TIME
10 minutes

COOKING TIME
50 minutes

INGREDIENTS
2¼ lb (1 kg) lamb, diced, trimmed of any fat or gristle
Good-quality olive oil
1 medium white onion, finely chopped
1 tbsp good-quality *herbes de Provence* plus extra for sprinkling
Splash of red wine
14 oz (400 g) tomato sauce
¾ cup veal or beef stock
4 oz (120 g) cherry tomatoes
½ bunch of fresh basil leaves, shredded

ACCEPTABLE FOR
RAPID WEIGHT LOSS
and
WEIGHT CONTROL

1 Season the lamb with a pinch of salt, and drizzle with a little olive oil. Cook the lamb in a hot frying pan for 2 minutes, browning and sealing on all sides. Remove from the pan and put into a colander to drain any excess liquid.

2 Heat a large, heavy-based saucepan over high heat, and add the lamb, a splash of red wine (enough to cover the meat), onion, the 1 tbsp *herbes de Provence*, tomato sauce, and veal stock. Reduce the heat to medium and simmer, uncovered, for 45 minutes.

3 To prepare the tomatoes, preheat the oven to 400°F (200°C). Place the tomatoes in a single layer in a roasting pan and drizzle with olive oil, then sprinkle with salt and the extra *herbes de Provence*. Roast in the oven for 4–5 minutes—the tomato skins should blister and crack. Keep warm.

4 When the lamb is cooked, transfer the stew to a ceramic serving dish. Sprinkle with the basil and cherry tomatoes. Drizzle any of the tomato cooking juices over the top. Serve hot.

SERVES 4

PREPARATION TIME
10 minutes

COOKING TIME
10 minutes

INGREDIENTS

1 tsp butter

6 shallots, finely chopped

½ bottle red wine

3½ tbsp red wine vinegar

1 cup beef stock

4 entrecôte steaks (ask your butcher to cut these for you) or good-quality sirloin, trimmed of excess fat or gristle

Olive oil

3 oz (100 g) ceps, trimmed and sliced (if you are using dried ceps, soften in hot water for 20 minutes first)

3 oz (100 g) bone marrow, cut into ½-in (1-cm) rounds (available from high-end butcher shops) (optional)

2 oz (50 g) chopped fresh parsley

ACCEPTABLE FOR

RAPID WEIGHT LOSS

and

WEIGHT CONTROL

Entrecôte steaks, Bordeaux style

Entrecôte is a cut of beef taken from between the ninth and eleventh ribs of the animal. Hardly surprising, since *entrecôte* is French for "between the ribs." Supremely tender, this type of steak responds best to minimal cooking.

1   To prepare the red wine sauce, heat a heavy-based saucepan over high heat. Drop in the butter and add the shallot. Sweat for a couple of minutes, until softened, then add the wine and red wine vinegar. Bring to the boil and reduce the liquid by two-thirds. Add the stock and keep reducing until the consistency of a sauce. Remove from the heat, add salt to taste, and leave in a warm place.

2   If using the marrow, bring a small saucepan of salted water to a boil. Season the steaks with salt and pepper to taste. Drizzle a little olive oil into a frying pan over high heat. When smoking hot, add the steaks and quickly sear on each side, until medium. Remove from the pan and set on a plate or tray to rest.

3   Reduce the heat under the pan to medium, and add the ceps. Cook briskly for about 3 minutes, then add the red wine sauce, stirring to deglaze the pan. Remove from the heat and keep warm.

4   Carefully drop the marrow, if using, into the pan of boiling water and poach for 30 seconds. At serving time, the marrow will slip easily out of the bone.

5   To serve, put a steak on each of 4 warmed serving plates. Spoon on the red wine sauce with mushrooms. Add the marrow, if using, and sprinkle on the parsley. Serve immediately.

SERVES 4

PREPARATION TIME
20 minutes, plus at least
12 hours for marinating

COOKING TIME
5 hours

INGREDIENTS
3½ lb (1.5 kg) lean braising
steak, cut into 1-in (2-cm)
cubes

1 onion, sliced

2 garlic cloves, finely
chopped

Zest of 1 orange, cut into
strips

Sprig of fresh rosemary, a
couple of stalks of parsley
and a bay leaf tied into a
bouquet garni

2½ cups red wine

1 tbsp olive oil

4 oz (120 g) smoked bacon
lardons

3 celery sticks

1 bunch of fresh thyme
leaves

1¼ cups beef stock

2 oz (60 g) black olives,
pitted

ACCEPTABLE FOR
RAPID WEIGHT LOSS
and
WEIGHT CONTROL

Daube de boeuf

Another slow-cooking method which makes meat as tender
as possible, daubes are common throughout France. A heavy
clay casserole dish known as a *daubière* is often used for this
dish, but any deep ovenproof dish with a lid will do.

1   Put the steak cubes into a large bowl or dish, add half the onion
    and the garlic, orange zest, bouquet garni, and wine. Marinate in the
    refrigerator for several hours, preferably overnight.

2   Preheat the oven to 250°F (130°C). Drain the beef, reserving the
    marinade. Heat the olive oil in a large, deep, heatproof casserole dish
    over high heat. Brown the lardons. Add the rest of the onion and
    the celery, and sweat for a couple of minutes, until softened.

3   Now add the beef and brown on all sides, before adding the garlic,
    thyme, orange zest from the marinade, and about 2 tbsp of the
    marinade itself. Stir, scraping any sediment from the bottom of the
    casserole, then strain the remainder of the marinade liquid into the
    casserole dish. Pour in the stock and add salt and freshly ground
    black pepper to taste.

4   Place a sheet of parchment paper over the top of the casserole dish,
    then cover with the lid. Braise in the oven for 4–5 hours. Remove
    the lid and parchment paper, and skim off any fat. Now add the
    olives, place the casserole dish over high heat, and reduce the
    cooking liquid to a sauce, with the lid off. Serve hot.

SERVES 4

PREPARATION TIME
15 minutes

COOKING TIME
11 minutes

INGREDIENTS
7 oz (200 g) French beans
(young green beans)
1 lb (450 g) rump steak
1 red onion, halved
Good-quality olive oil
3 oz (85 g) baby leaf spinach
2 oz (50 g) watercress
7 oz (200 g) dried tomatoes
in oil, drained

HORSERADISH SAUCE
½ cup plain yogurt
1 tbsp horseradish cream
2 tbsp lemon juice
2 tbsp heavy cream
2 garlic cloves, thinly sliced
2–3 drops of Tabasco sauce

ACCEPTABLE FOR
RAPID WEIGHT LOSS
and
WEIGHT CONTROL

Broiled beef with spinach and horseradish sauce

Tender, succulent slices of broiled beef are served here with a fresh salad and a variation of horseradish sauce, a traditional accompaniment to that old British standard, roast beef. The sauce adds a kick of tangy lemon and a fiery hint of Tabasco.

1 Steam the French beans for about 4 minutes, until tender. Set aside.

2 Preheat the broiler. When it is hot, brush the beef and the onion with some olive oil. Broil the meat for 2 minutes on each side, and set aside to rest for 5 minutes. Meanwhile, broil the onion for 3 minutes on each side.

3 Arrange the spinach, watercress, tomatoes, and beans on a serving platter.

4 To make the horseradish sauce, beat together the yogurt, horseradish cream, lemon juice, cream, garlic, Tabasco sauce, and salt and freshly ground black pepper to taste.

5 Cut the beef into thin slices and arrange over the salad. Slice the onion thinly and sprinkle it over the dish. Add the horseradish sauce and serve. Alternatively, serve on individual plates, with the salad topping the beef, rather than the other way around, and a spoonful of the horseradish sauce drizzled over the top.

SERVES 4

PREPARATION TIME
15 minutes

COOKING TIME
20 minutes

INGREDIENTS
4 veal fillets or veal loins,
about 6 oz (150 g) each
Olive oil

GORGONZOLA SAUCE
1 tbsp heavy cream plus
3 tbsp extra, whipped
2 tbsp veal or beef stock
1½ tbsp sherry vinegar
3 tbsp dry sherry
⅔ cup cubed Gorgonzola
cheese

ACCEPTABLE FOR
  RAPID WEIGHT LOSS
and
  WEIGHT CONTROL

Veal fillet in Gorgonzola sauce

Veal fillet works wonderfully here, but it can be expensive, so you may prefer to use veal tenderloin instead. Whichever you choose, the creamy yet light sauce, redolent of the flavor of Gorgonzola, manages to be the perfect accompaniment.

1 Preheat the oven to 400°F (200°C).

2 To make the sauce, bring the stock, cream, sherry vinegar, and sherry to a boil in a heavy-based saucepan. Simmer until the sauce is reduced to two-thirds of its original volume.

3 Drop in the Gorgonzola a little at a time, using a hand-held electric mixer to whisk the cheese into the sauce. Once smooth, strain the sauce through a fine sieve, then add the whipped cream and stir through gently. Set aside to keep warm.

4 Heat a little olive oil in a frying pan over medium heat and brown the veal on both sides. Transfer to a casserole dish and cook in the oven for 6–8 minutes. Remove from the oven and allow to rest in a warm place for 5 minutes before cutting into thick slices, or you can leave them whole if you wish.

5 Divide the veal among 4 serving plates, top each serving with a little of the Gorgonzola sauce, and serve.

Pork chops in caper sauce

A simple dry rub is used to coat these pork chops before they are cooked. Topped with a fresh caper sauce that is bursting with the flavors of capers, tomato, lemon, and parsley, they are a fast way to put a meal on the table.

SERVES 4

PREPARATION TIME
10 minutes

COOKING TIME
16 minutes

INGREDIENTS
2 tbsp ground almonds
1 tsp paprika
½ tsp salt
½ tsp cracked black pepper
Good-quality olive oil
4 pork chops, about ½ lb (120 g) each
8 capers to garnish

CAPER SAUCE
1 very ripe tomato, halved, seeded, and diced
1 tbsp drained capers, rinsed and squeezed
2 tbsp chopped fresh parsley
3 tbsp olive oil
Juice of 1 lemon

ACCEPTABLE FOR
RAPID WEIGHT LOSS
and
WEIGHT CONTROL

1 Combine the ground almonds, paprika, salt, and pepper in a bowl or on a plate. Use to lightly coat the pork chops on both sides.

2 Drizzle a little olive oil into a frying pan over medium heat. When hot, cook the chops for 8 minutes on each side, or until tender.

3 To make the caper sauce, mix the tomato, capers, parsley, olive oil, and lemon juice. Add salt and freshly ground black pepper to taste.

4 Place a pork chop on each of 4 warm serving plates, and cover each serving with a spoonful of the caper sauce. Garnish with the capers and serve immediately.

SERVES 4

COOKING TIME
45 minutes, plus at least
1 hour for marinating

INGREDIENTS
2¼ lb (1 kg) diced pork,
trimmed of fat and rinsed
under cold water

2 tsp dry white wine

2 tsp white wine vinegar

A few whole black
peppercorns

2 bay leaves (fresh is best)

1 celeriac bulb, peeled and
diced

3 leeks, cut into rings

1 onion, chopped

1 cup chicken stock

3 or 4 apples, cut into 6
segments and core removed

2 tbsp fructose

1 tbsp butter

4 oz (100 g) pitted prunes

1 tsp lemon juice

1 tsp Dijon mustard

2 tbsp chopped fresh parsley

ACCEPTABLE FOR
RAPID WEIGHT LOSS
and
WEIGHT CONTROL

Pork with apples and prunes

This pork dish is similar to a fricassee, but the vegetables with which the meat is stewed are blended to a smooth sauce at the end of cooking. The final touch is a topping of caramelized apples and prunes, which provide a contrasting sweetness.

1 Put the pork in a glass or ceramic dish with the white wine, vinegar, peppercorns, and 1 bay leaf. Marinate in the refrigerator for at least 1 hour, preferably overnight.

2 Transfer the drained pork to a large, heavy-based saucepan and cook over high heat for 2 minutes, or until colored, turning frequently to seal on all sides. Remove from the pan and set aside.

3 Reduce the heat to medium and, using the same pan, sweat the celeriac, leek, and onion for 2–3 minutes, until softened. Add 1 bay leaf and the stock. Return the pork to the pan, cover with a lid, and stew for a further 40 minutes, stirring from time to time.

4 Place the apple segments in large buttered frying pan over a high heat. Add the fructose and the butter. Caramelize the apple for 6 minutes, then add the prunes. Keep warm until needed.

5 Remove the pork from the vegetables and reserve. Blend or process the vegetable mixture, including the liquid but minus the bay leaf, for a few minutes, until smooth. Return to the pan to reheat.

6 Add the meat to the sauce, stir through, and transfer to a casserole dish to serve. Top with the caramelized apples and prunes as a garnish. Sprinkle on the parsley and serve hot.

SERVES 4

PREPARATION TIME
10 minutes

COOKING TIME
20 minutes

INGREDIENTS
2 tsp drained capers
Good-quality olive oil
5 shallots, finely chopped
1½ tbsp white wine
1¼ cups veal or
beef stock
¾ cup crème fraîche or sour
cream
1 tsp whole-grain mustard
½ tsp Dijon mustard
½ bunch of chopped fresh
tarragon or chives
1 tbsp goose fat or olive oil
4 pork chops or pork
tenderloins, about ¼ lb
(100 g) each

ACCEPTABLE FOR
RAPID WEIGHT LOSS

and

WEIGHT CONTROL

Pork with herbed mustard

A creamy, herb-infused mustard sauce is used to smother thick, succulent pork chops in this recipe. The pork is cooked in a little goose fat to help the meat retain its moisture, but you can substitute olive oil if you prefer.

1 Put the capers into a small colander and rinse with cold water (to get rid of the brine and/or vinegar in which they have been preserved). Squeeze until they are almost dry.

2 Heat a small saucepan over high heat and drizzle the pan with a little olive oil. Add the shallot, white wine, capers, and stock. Bring to a boil and reduce the liquid for 12–15 minutes, until it is about a third of its original volume.

3 Whisk in the crème fraîche, then add the whole-grain and Dijon mustards. Sprinkle in the tarragon. Keep the sauce warm.

4 While you are cooking the sauce, heat a large frying pan over a medium heat. Melt the goose fat in the pan, then add the pork. Cook the meat for 6–8 minutes on each side, until golden.

5 Drain the chops on paper towels, to absorb any excess fat. Place a chop on each of 4 serving plates, spoon on the mustard sauce, and serve immediately.

Desserts

All of the desserts in this section are acceptable as part of the Rapid Weight Loss plan and the Weight Control plan. The decadent chocolate cake (*see pp232-33*) is a favorite low-GI treat at the Montignac Boutique & Café in London. Now, for the first time, the Café shares its popular recipes with you, so you too can enjoy delicious, guilt-free desserts at home.

Chocolate cake

This cake shows the benefit of using top-quality ingredients—in this case, chocolate. The secret here is to have your oven as hot as possible and to work quickly once your chocolate has melted. The result is a rich but not overpowering delight.

SERVES 6–8

PREPARATION TIME
30 minutes, plus overnight refrigeration

COOKING TIME
8 minutes

INGREDIENTS
11 oz (310 g) dark chocolate (70 percent cocoa solids), broken into pieces, plus extra 7 oz (185 g) for topping
10 large eggs, separated

ACCEPTABLE FOR
RAPID WEIGHT LOSS
and
WEIGHT CONTROL

1 Line an 8-in (20-cm) round springform pan with baking parchment. The collar lining the side of the pan should rise an inch or so (a few centimeters) above the top of the pan. Preheat the oven to 500°F (250°C).

2 Place a large, clean, dry bowl over a saucepan of simmering water, making sure the bowl does not touch the water. Put the 11 oz (310 g) chocolate in the bowl to melt (about 15–20 minutes), stirring often.

3 Put the egg whites in a large bowl and, using a hand-held electric mixer, beat until stiff peaks form. Do not overbeat.

4 Transfer the bowl with the melted chocolate from the pan to a work surface. Gently stir the beaten egg yolks into the chocolate. Add a couple of tablespoons of the egg white and stir just to combine. Quickly and gently fold in the rest of the egg white until the mixture has the consistency of a soufflé or light mousse. Do not overmix.

5 Pour the chocolate mixture into the pan and bake in the oven for 8 minutes exactly. Remove the pan from the oven and cool for 30 minutes, then chill in the refrigerator for 12 hours or overnight.

6 To finish, take the cake out of the refrigerator and turn out onto a large plate or a piece of plastic wrap on a flat work surface. Melt the extra chocolate in the same way as in Step 2. Pour a thin film of chocolate over the cake. Chill in the refrigerator for 5 minutes. To serve, dip a sharp knife in hot water and use to slice the cake.

Peach mousse

Choose the ripest, sweetest, and most fragrant peaches you can find for this light and fluffy mousse—but watch out for bruising. It is better to choose a peach variety with colored flesh, so that these shades are carried into the finished mousse.

SERVES 4

PREPARATION TIME
20 minutes

COOKING TIME
5 minutes

INGREDIENTS
2 sheets leaf gelatin or ½ envelope powdered gelatin

1 lb (450 g) peaches, peeled, cored and quartered

¼ cup fructose plus a little extra for sweetening

Juice of ½ lemon

2 eggs, separated

1 tbsp heavy cream

1 tsp vanilla extract

ACCEPTABLE FOR
 RAPID WEIGHT LOSS

and

 WEIGHT CONTROL

1   If using leaf gelatin, soak the gelatin in cold water.

2   Using an electric mixer, blend the peaches with half the fructose and the lemon juice. Push through a fine sieve or strainer into a bowl.

3   Beat the egg yolks in a bowl with the remaining fructose until light and fluffy. Heat gently over a saucepan of simmering water, until the fructose has dissolved and the mixture coats the back of a spoon. Remove the bowl from the heat and allow to cool.

4   Drain the soaked gelatin of any cold water, if using leaf gelatin, then pour 2 tbsp hot water over the sheets or gelatin powder. Whisk the melted or dissolved gelatin into the peach mixture. Pour in the cooled egg yolk mixture, and continue whisking until smooth.

5   Whisk the egg whites until stiff peaks form. In a separate small bowl, whip the cream until firm, adding the vanilla extract and a little extra fructose to sweeten slightly.

6   Gently fold the cream into the peach mixture, then gently fold in the egg whites, one-third at a time, using a spatula—do not stir, because you want to keep as much air as possible in the mixture so that your mousse is light and fluffy.

7   Chill in the refrigerator for at least 4 hours before serving in individual parfait glasses or ice cream dishes.

Chocolate vanilla pots

SERVES 4

PREPARATION TIME
10 minutes, plus 10 or so
hours for chilling

COOKING TIME
15 minutes

INGREDIENTS

CHOCOLATE MOUSSE
9 oz (260 g) dark chocolate
chips (preferably 70 percent
cocoa solids)
1 cup heavy cream
1 cup milk
2 large eggs, beaten

VANILLA CREAM
2½ cups heavy cream
1 vanilla pod, split lengthwise
9 large egg yolks
¼ cup fructose

Whipped cream to decorate
Chocolate flakes to decorate

ACCEPTABLE FOR
  RAPID WEIGHT LOSS
and
  WEIGHT CONTROL

These chocolate vanilla pots look very tempting with their layers of chocolate and vanilla. And they are all the more tempting on the palate. If you have extra mousse after filling your serving glasses, simply make up another pot.

1   To make the chocolate mousse, put the chocolate chips into a blender or food processor. Pour the heavy cream and milk into a small, heavy-based saucepan. Bring to a boil carefully—do not scorch.

2   When the cream mixture has just come to a boil, turn on the blender or processor, and pour in the hot cream mixture. Add the eggs and blend until smooth. Fill 4 individual glasses or glass serving dishes to the halfway point. Cover with plastic wrap and chill in the refrigerator for about 8 hours to set.

3   To make the vanilla cream, pour the cream into a medium, heavy-based saucepan. Scrape the seeds from the vanilla pod into the cream. Bring carefully to just below the boil.

4   In the meantime, put the egg yolks into a bowl with the fructose, and whisk until combined. Add some of the warm cream and quickly mix. Pour the egg mixture into the pan with the rest of the cream. Cook, stirring with a wooden spoon, until it thickens and coats the back of the spoon. Strain and chill for at least 2 hours.

5   When the chocolate mousse has set, pour the vanilla cream on top. Fill the glasses almost to the rim, so that you have a layer of chocolate and a layer of vanilla cream. Chill until ready to serve.

6   Serve topped with a swirl of whipped cream and a sprinkle of chocolate flakes.

SERVES 4

PREPARATION TIME
20 minutes, plus at least
4 hours for chilling

COOKING TIME
0 minutes

INGREDIENTS
6 oz (150 g) dark chocolate
(preferably 70 percent cocoa
solids), broken into pieces

1 tbsp heavy cream, at room
temperature

8 oz (225 g) raspberries,
crushed

4 large eggs, separated

ACCEPTABLE FOR
RAPID WEIGHT LOSS
and
WEIGHT CONTROL

Raspberry and chocolate mousse

Chocolate and raspberries are an almost symbiotic pairing. Their flavors are set off well in this simple mousse. As with all mousses, the secret to the right result is to fold in the egg whites, not stir. The latter flattens your mousse.

1 Melt the chocolate in a bowl set over a saucepan of simmering water, making sure the bowl does not touch the water. Allow to cool and stir in the cream.

2 Beat the egg yolks and add to the chocolate mixture, then stir in the crushed raspberries.

3 Beat the egg whites until firm peaks form. Gently fold into the chocolate mixture, a third at a time, using a spatula. Be careful not to overmix, since this will take all the lightness out of your mousse.

4 Pour the mousse into a glass or ceramic serving dish, or 4 individual dishes. Chill in the refrigerator for at least 4 hours before serving.

REFERENCE

GI chart: high to low

This glycemic index lists its entries from high to low. Use this chart to find out which foods have high GI values so that you can avoid them. Entries marked with an asterisk have a low concentration of carbohydrates (see p115), which means you can eat them in moderation on the Weight Control plan.

Maltose (beer)	110	Chocolate bar, milk chocolate	70
Glucose (dextrose)	100	Cola drinks	70
Potatoes (fried or French fries)	95	Corn starch	70
Potatoes (peeled; baked)	95	Potatoes (peeled; boiled)	70
Rice (instant)	90	Ravioli; tortellini	70
Puffed rice	85	Rice (parboiled, nonstick)	70
Honey	85	Risotto rice	70
Carrots (cooked)	85	Sugar (sucrose)	70
Cornflakes	85	Beets	65
Flour, refined, white	85	Brown flour	65
Popcorn (no sugar added)	85	Corn (fresh; steamed)	65
Pretzels	85	Couscous (cooked for five minutes)	65
Rice cakes	85	Golden raisins	65
Tapioca	85	Jam (with sugar)	65
Turnips*	85	Orange juice (commercial variety)	65
Crackers (made from white flour)	80	Potatoes (baked; skin on)	65
Potato chips	80	Potatoes (boiled; skin on)	65
Potatoes (mashed)	80	Raisins	65
Flour, refined, white (bread flour)	75	Sherbet (with sugar)	65
Pumpkin*	75	Bananas (ripe)	60
Watermelon*	75	Melon *	60
Cereals (refined)	70	Semolina (white, cooked)	60

Rice (long-grain; white)	60	Unrefined flour, whole-wheat	40
Shortbread cookies	55	Apples (dried)	35
Petit beurre cookies	55	Apricots (dried)	35
White pasta, soft-wheat (cooked well)	55	Beans, fava (peeled and cooked)	35
All-bran	50	Beans, haricot	35
Apple juice (fresh)	50	Figs (fresh)	35
Crêpes (made with buckwheat)	50	Ice cream (made with alginates)	35
Kiwi fruit	50	Kidney beans	35
Rice (unrefined basmati)	50	Oranges	35
Rice (brown)	50	Natural yogurt	35
Sweet potatoes	50	Peas, dried (cooked)	35
Unrefined flour	50	Peas, fresh (cooked)	35
Buckwheat	45	Plums	35
Bulgur wheat (whole-grain, cooked)	45	Prunes	35
Grapes (all kinds)	45	Quinoa	35
Orange juice (freshly squeezed)	45	Clementines	35
Pasta (made from pasta flour)	45	Wild rice	35
Whole-wheat bread with bran	45	Apples (fresh)	30
Black bread (German)	40	Apricots (fresh)	30
Figs (dried)	40	Beans, French	30
Sherbet (sugar-free)	40	Carrots (raw)	30
Spaghetti, durum-wheat (cooked al dente)	40	Chickpeas (cooked)	30
Spaghetti, whole-wheat (cooked al dente)	40	Garlic	30
Rye bread (whole-grain)	40	Grapefruit	30
Unrefined bread flour	40	Jam (sugar-free)	30

GI chart: high to low

Lentils (brown)	30		Brazil nuts	15
Lentils (red)	30		Pumpkin seeds	15
Lentils (yellow)	30		Sunflower seeds	15
Milk (reduced-fat or skim)	30		Olives (all kinds)	15
Mung beans (soaked and cooked for 20 minutes)	30		Asparagus	15
Nectarines	30		Artichokes	15
Peaches	30		Broccoli	15
Pears	30		Brussels sprouts	15
Tomatoes	30		Cabbage (all kinds)	15
Beans, flageolet	25		Cauliflower	15
Cherries	25		Celeriac	15
Dark chocolate (70 percent cocoa)	25		Celery	15
Lentils (green)	25		Cucumber	15
Strawberries	25		Fennel	15
Blackberries	25		Herbs	15
Raspberries	25		Leeks	15
Soybeans (cooked)	25		Lettuce (all kinds)	15
Split peas (yellow, cooked for 20 minutes)	25		Mushrooms	15
Chinese vermicelli (soybean variety)	22		Peanuts	15
Eggplant	20		Peppers (all colours and varieties)	15
Fructose	20		Onions (all kinds)	15
Lemons	20		Spinach	15
Limes	20		Zucchini	15
Almonds, walnuts, hazelnuts	15		Avocados	10
Pecans	15			

GI chart: alphabetical order

This glycemic index lists its entries in alphabetical order. Use this chart when you know the name of a carbohydrate, but don't know its GI value. Entries marked with an asterisk have a low concentration of carbohydrates (see p115), which means you can eat them in moderation on the Weight Control plan.

All-bran	50	Buckwheat	45
Almonds, walnuts, hazelnuts	15	Bulgur wheat (whole-grain, cooked)	45
Apples (dried)	35	Cabbage (all kinds)	15
Apples (fresh)	30	Carrots (cooked)*	85
Apple juice (fresh)	50	Carrots (raw)	30
Apricots (dried)	35	Cauliflower	15
Apricots (fresh)	30	Celeriac	15
Artichokes	15	Celery	15
Asparagus	15	Cereals (refined)	70
Avocados	10	Cherries	25
Bananas (ripe)	60	Chickpeas (cooked)	30
Beans, fava (peeled and cooked)	35	Chinese vermicelli (soybean variety)	22
Beans, flageolet	25	Clementines	35
Beans, French	30	Chocolate bar, milk chocolate	70
Beans, haricot	35	Cola drinks	70
Beets	65	Cornflakes	85
Blackberries	25	Corn starch	70
Black bread (German)	40	Corn (fresh; steamed)	65
Brazil nuts	15	Couscous (cooked for five minutes	65
Broccoli	15	Crêpes (made with buckwheat)	50
Brown flour	65	Crackers (made from white flour)	80
Brussels sprouts	15	Cucumber	15

GI chart: alphabetical order

Dark chocolate (70 percent cocoa)	25	Lentils (yellow)	30
Eggplant	20	Lettuce (all kinds)	15
Fennel	15	Maltose (beer)	110
Figs (dried)	40	Melon*	60
Figs (fresh)	35	Milk (reduced-fat or skim)	30
Flour, refined, white	85	Mung beans (soaked and cooked for 20 minutes)	30
Fructose	20	Mushrooms	15
Garlic	30	Natural yogurt	35
Glucose (dextrose)	100	Nectarines	30
Golden raisins	65	Olives (all kinds)	15
Grapefruit	30	Onions (all kinds)	15
Grapes (all kinds)	45	Oranges	35
Herbs	15	Orange juice (commercial variety)	65
Honey	85	Orange juice (freshly squeezed)	45
Ice cream (made with alginates)	35	Pasta (made from whole-wheat flour)	45
Jam (made with sugar)	65	Peaches	30
Jam (sugar-free)	30	Peanuts	15
Kidney beans	35	Pears	30
Kiwi fruit	50	Peas, dried (cooked)	35
Leeks	15	Peas, fresh (cooked)	35
Lemons	20	Pecans	15
Limes	20	Peppers (all colors and varieties)	15
Lentils (brown)	30	Petit beurre cookies	55
Lentils (green)	25	Plums	35
Lentils (red)	30	Popcorn (no sugar added)	85

Potato chips	80	Sherbet (sugar-free)	40
Potatoes (baked; skin on)	65	Sherbet (with sugar)	65
Potatoes (boiled; skin on)	65	Shortbread cookies	55
Potatoes (fried or French fries)	95	Soybeans (cooked)	25
Potatoes (mashed)	80	Spaghetti, durum-wheat (cooked *al dente*)	40
Potatoes (peeled; baked)	95	Spaghetti, whole-wheat (cooked *al dente*)	40
Potatoes (peeled; boiled)	70	Spinach	15
Prunes	35	Split peas (yellow, cooked for 20 minutes)	25
Puffed rice	85	Strawberries	25
Pumpkin*	75	Sugar (sucrose)	70
Pumpkin seeds	15	Sunflower seeds	15
Pretzels	85	Sweet potatoes	50
Raisins	65	Tapioca	85
Raspberries	25	Tomatoes	30
Ravioli; tortellini	70	Turnips*	85
Rice (brown)	50	Unrefined flour, whole-wheat	50
Rice (unrefined basmati)	50	Watermelon*	75
Rice cakes	85	White pasta, soft-wheat (cooked well)	55
Rice (long-grain; white)	60	Whole-wheat bread with bran	45
Rice (instant)	90	Wild rice	35
Rice (parboiled)	70	Zucchini	15
Risotto rice	70		
Rye bread (whole-grain)	40		
Quinoa	35		
Semolina (white, cooked)	60		

Glossary

antioxidant
An enzyme or other organic molecule that can counteract the damaging effects of free radicals in the body.

AGI
Stands for the Average Glycemic Index, which is the resulting GI of two or more carbohydrates of differing GI values when eaten together.

carbohydrates
Also termed sugars, carbohydrates are the body's primary source of fuel. Carbohydrates are metabolized by the body into glucose, which acts as an important source of energy.

concentration of carbohydrates
The number of grams of carbohydrates a food contains per 3.5-oz (100-gram) serving.

diabetes type II
A chronic metabolic disorder that occurs when the body's cells become immune to insulin secreted by the pancreas. In many cases, the condition must be regulated with drugs.

discrepancy
A planned deviation from the Diet that allows you to eat the occasional dessert, serving of French fries, or other food with a GI significantly higher than 50.

You are allowed two discrepancies per month on the Weight Control plan. Discrepancies are not allowed on the Rapid Weight Loss plan.

fats
Complex molecules that store energy for long-term use by the body; also called fatty acids.

fructose
A naturally occurring fruit sugar with a low GI of 20. Fructose is thermostable, which means it retains its sweetness when heated and can be used in cooking and baking.

glucose
The sugar into which the body converts carbohydrates; also a syrup made from corn starch that is added to foods as a sweetener.

glycemia
The level of glucose in the blood; another term for blood sugar level.

glycemic index (GI)
A system that measures the amount of sugar a food contains and the effect it will have on blood sugar levels. Each food is assigned a number, which tells you comparatively, gram for gram, how much sugar a food contains, and how much of it will be absorbed by the body.

glycogen

Glucose that is converted into a short-term energy source and is stored in the muscles of the body. When blood sugar levels fall below normal, the body converts stored glycogen back into glucose.

hyperglycemia

An acute condition marked by extremely high blood sugar levels. This is caused by eating high-GI foods, which, in turn, triggers the pancreas to release a large amount of insulin to bring the blood sugar levels down to normal.

hyperinsulinism

A chronic metabolic condition in which the pancreas is very sensitive to glucose, releasing more—sometimes much more—insulin than is required in response to a carbohydrate.

hypoglycemia

An acute condition in which an excess of insulin in the blood causes abnormally low blood sugar levels. Symptoms include fatigue, lack of concentration, intense hunger, and irritability.

insulin

A hormone secreted by the pancreas, which drives sugar in the form of glucose out of the bloodstream and into the body's cells.

pancreas

An organ that produces enzymes that assist in digestion, and also produces hormones such as insulin, which helps the body use sugar for energy.

pastification

A mechanical process in which pasta dough is fed through small holes at a very high pressure. This gives the pastas, such as spaghetti, a protective film, which limits the amount of starch released during the cooking process and lowers the GI value by about five points.

protein

Organic substances that are found in a wide variety of animal and vegetable foods, particularly meat, fish, chicken, eggs, and soy products. Proteins contain large amounts of amino acids, which are used to make cells.

retrogradation

Also known as the cooling process, retrogradation can reduce the GI of some cooked carbohydrates, particularly pasta.

saturated fat

Saturated fat is solid at room temperature, and may contribute to cardiovascular disease. It is mainly derived from animal sources, such as fatty cuts of meat and butter.

unsaturated fat

Unsaturated fat is liquid at room temperature, and it does not contribute to cardiovascular disease. Some unsaturated fats (polyunsaturated fats, found mainly in fish) may even lower blood cholesterol levels. Unsaturated fats are derived mainly from vegetable sources, such as olive oil, and oily fish, such as salmon and tuna.

Useful resources

General information

www.montignac.com

The Montignac Universal Official Website, complete with detailed information about the science behind the Diet, extensive GI listings, Montignac product information, and a forum for questions and advice about the Diet.

For natural and organic foods

Whole Foods Market is the world's largest retailer of natural and organic foods, including arabica coffee, whole-grain bread, whole-wheat pasta, seeds, nuts, sugar-free fruit preserves, and a wide variety of beans, grains, and fructose. There are over 155 Whole Foods Markets throughout North America and the United Kingdom.
www.wholefoodsmarket.com

For low-carbohydrate, low-GI food products

www.low-carbshop.com

For specialty foods

Gourmet Garage
www.gourmetgarage.com

Dean & Deluca
www.deandeluca.com

Eli's Vinegar Factory
www.elismanhattan.com
(212) 987-0885
Fresh Direct
www.freshdirect.com

www.HealthyGourmetStore.com

For buying goose fat

www.ChefShop.com

For foie gras, paté, duck confit, etc.

Frenchy Bee Gourmet
www.frenchybee.com

For game meat, foie gras, paté, and specialty sausages, etc.

D'Artagnan
www.dartagnan.com

Information on diabetes

Canadian Diabetes Association
National Life Building
1400-522 University Avenue
Toronto, Ontario Canada M5G 2R5
Tel: (800) 226-8464
www.diabetes.ca

American Diabetes Association
1701 North Beauregard Street
Alexandria, VA 22311
Tel: (800) DIABETES
www.diabetes.org

Information on a healthy diet

Dietitians of Canada
480 University Avenue, Suite 604
Toronto, Ontario, Canada M5G 1V2
Tel: (416)-596-0857
www.dietitians.ca

American Dietetic Association
1201 South Riverside Plaza
Suite 2000
Chicago, IL 60606-6995
Tel: (800) 877-1600
www.eatright.org

Information on organic food

Organic Consumers Association
6101 Cliff Estate Road
Little Marais, MN 55614
Tel: (218) 226-4164
www.organicconsumers.org

Recommended reading by the same author

The Montignac Method Just for Children
(Montignac Publishing Ltd., 2004)

Montignac Provençal Cookbook
(Montignac Publishing Ltd., 2002)

Eat Well, Stay Young
(Montignac Publishing Ltd., 2001)

Eat Yourself Slim and Stay Slim
(Montignac Publishing Ltd., 1999)

The Miracle of Wine
(Montignac Publishing Ltd., 1997)

Dine Out and Lose Weight
(Montignac Publishing Ltd., 1996)

The Montignac Method Just for Women
(Montignac Publishing Ltd., 1995)

Montignac Recipes and Menus
(Montignac Publishing Ltd., 1993)

Index

Acknowledgments

AUTHOR'S ACKNOWLEDGMENTS

Michel Montignac would like to say a special thanks to: Suzy, my darling wife who graciously gave up parties and weekends during the writing of this book to help me find the appropriate words and expressions; Mónica Lalinde, my assistant, whose computer expertise was especially valuable to me as I am still a beginner in this area; Ernest Hilton, the manager and owner of the Montignac Boutique & Café (gourmet food store, café, and wine bar at 160 Old Brompton Road, London, England), who has become an expert on my diet, and who supplied the recipes for this book; Shannon Beatty, my editor at DK, who spent many late nights and weekends working on this project; Jenny Jones at DK, who also devoted a great deal of her time to this book; Jo Grey for the beautiful book design; and Mary-Clare Jerram for her unwavering support for this book.

PUBLISHER'S ACKNOWLEDGMENTS

Dorling Kindersley would like to thank Kate Whitaker for photography; Luis Peral for art direction; home economist Valerie Berry for making the recipes camera-ready; Penny Markham for the styling; Siobhan O'Connor for editing the recipes; Ernest Hilton for providing the recipes; Diana Vowles for additional editorial assistance; Christine Heilman for editing the Canadian edition, and Valerie Chandler for compiling the index.

Picture credits

Laurie Evans 10–11, 25, 30–31, 33, 47, 58–59, 68–69, 238–39

Corbis: 27, 76–77, 98–99, 134–35

All other images © DK Images

ABOUT THE AUTHOR

World-renowned French diet guru Michel Montignac was born in southern France. Through his rigorous study of nutritional and scientific documents, he devised the Montignac Method, which helped him to lose 35 pounds in three months.

In 1986 he self-published his first book, *Eat Yourself Slim and Stay Slim*, the first-ever diet book based on the GI. His groundbreaking work (which has since been corroborated by numerous studies), states that it is not the restriction of calories, but the exclusion of high-GI carbohydrates and saturated fats that induces sustainable weight loss. He is the author of more than 20 books, which are available in more than 42 countries and 25 languages. Today, the GI is a hot topic, with many of the world's best-selling diet books based on his findings. Michel Montignac now lives in Geneva, where he devotes his time to research, writing, and lecturing.